KW-325-309

PLAYING WITH FIRE

A Natural Selection of Religious Poetry

0108382

Books are to be returned on or before
the last date below.

14. DEC

12. JAN 95

06. FEB

13. MAR

1 2 JUN 2000 CANCELLED

LIBREX —

BJ8976

PLAYING WITH FIRE

A natural selection of Religious Poetry

edited by Susan Dwyer

VILLA BOOKS
DUBLIN

SB 13340 /595. 5:80

First published by Villa Books in 1980
Villa Books Limited, 55 Dame Street, Dublin 2, Ireland
Copyright this collection © Susan Dwyer, 1980.
All rights reserved.
British Library Cataloguing in Publication Data
    Playing with fire
    1. Religious poetry
    I.   Dwyer, Susan
    808.81'5   PN6110.R4

ISBN 0-906408-12-1

Printed and bound in Great Britain by
Redwood Burn Limited
Trowbridge & Esher

The Questions of Ethne Alba

Who is God
and where is God,
of whom is God,
and where his dwelling?

Has he sons and daughters,
gold and silver, this God of yours?

Is he ever-living?
Is he beautiful,
was His son
fostered by many?

Are His daughters
dear and beautiful
to the men of the world?

Is he in heaven
or on the earth?
In the sea,
in the rivers,
in the mountains,
in the valleys?

Speak to us
tidings of Him:
How will He be seen,
how is He loved,
how is He found?

Is it in youth
or is it in old age
He is found?

*(trans. from the 17th - 18th century Irish
by James Carney)*

Editor's Note

This personal selection is an attempt to collect a broad sample of poetry from all ages which expresses man's relationship with the transcendent being we call God.

This, like all relationships, involves searching, doubt and sometimes non-belief as well as joy, delight, praise and peace. These poems are about such a relationship.

I would like to thank Veronica Brady, William Hart-Smith, Gerard Windsor and Fergus Mulligan for their helpful criticism and suggestions.

CONTENTS

CONTENTS

CONTENTS

CONTENTS

CONTENTS

CONTENTS

CONTENTS

CONTENTS

CONTENTS

CONTENTS

FOREWORD

Like any other good or bad Catholic I was brought up on hymns like 'Faith of our fathers' and 'Soul of my saviour'. I knew, long before I was instructed in literary criticism, that they were atrocious as art however unexceptionable they were as sincere expressions of devotion. It was, I assumed, sinful to scorn them. But a stage came in my aesthetic development when I was driven to say 'To hell with this' during a May Sunday service in the church of the Holy Name, Manchester. I could no longer tolerate those oleaginous tributes to Our Lady — 'Let us mingle together, voices joyful and glad' and so on — and I walked out. I had come to a realisation that bad religious art is a blasphemy, and that sincerity, like patriotism, is not enough. From that time on I have insisted on distinguishing between devotional para- or infra-literature and genuine religious literature, regarding the first as a commodity which the critic must leave alone lest he shock and impair the faith of the simple devout, and the second as no more separable from the main stream of literature than writing which takes love or politics or nature for its subject-matter. It is in order, as this anthology finely demonstrates, to compile a book of religious poetry, but we have to approach its contents in a very sceptical spirit. What I mean is that we do not require to be believers in order to assess its value as literature of belief. Better to give the reviewing of a book of religious verse to a sensitive atheist than to a boorish priest.

Devotional verse, like the hymns of Isaac Watts (some of which, however, touch real poetry), is judged by its capacity, when coupled to appropriate music, to find words for the lowest common denominator of faith.

17

Religious verse is more concerned with recording the
response of the individual soul, as opposed to the
motley congregation, to a religious experience. John
Donne, a very great religious poet, would cause scandal
if sung in a church or even at a football match. He treats
God too much like a lover, he invites rape and violence,
he makes jokes. His faith is almost terrifyingly in
evidence, whereas, paradoxically enough, devotional
verse must not show too much faith. It must use the
conventional forms of faith, which are cliches, matching
the ritual which, of its nature, has sooner or later had to
become *mere* ritual. The purpose of religious poetry is
to remind faith of its beginnings — in shock, in a wrestle
between acceptance and rejection, in a terrible remaking
of the world.

A characteristic of the greatest religious poetry is its
physicality or, if you like, its sacramentality. A sacram-
ent relates the world of the spirit to the world of bread,
wine, and water. A poet makes his apprehension of the
presence of God as sensuously immediate as the taste of
hot tea or a piece of ice thrust down the back of the
neck. This makes much religious poetry appear
blasphemous, but only to those who, never having had a
true religious experience, do not truly know what
religion is about. It is appropriate that this anthology
begins with an extract from the Canticles, or the Song
of Songs which is Solomon's. Theologians have told us
that this is an allegory of Christ's love for his Church,
but most secular readers have been content to take it as
a very sensuous, even sensual, epithalamium. If it is
really a religious allegory, then it is the finest of
religious allegories, since it combines the life of the
senses with an exaltation so mysterious and so intense
that it can only be of divine origin. Of course, it is
possible to interpret that 'divine' as referring to a numen

neither Christian nor Hebraic, to, in fact, Dionysus or
Venus or Amor. But that does not make the poem any
less religious, and it is only the presence of the exalta-
tion that enables us to describe it as a Christian allegory.

St John of the Cross borrows freely from the Song of
Songs in his own poem about the *noche oscura*. When
living in Gibraltar I set that poem in a verse-speaking
contest for children taught by the Christian Brothers.
The poem was swiftly and hotly rejected by Brothers
McQuaid and Murphy as being dangerous to young souls
not yet capable of perceiving it as a mystical allegory.
They were right perhaps, though their imputation that I
had committed the Sin against the Holy Ghost in
choosing San Juan de la Cruz undoubtedly went too far.
But there is a general implication to be drawn from their
fear and anger, and that is that most religious poetry
tends to be dangerous because it tends to be ambiguous.
A great religious poem records an experience of great
intensity and expresses it, since that is the way of great
poetry, through imagery drawn from the senses. Poetry
of its nature cannot deal with the reality, the *entitas
eschatologica* which, unexpectedly, seemingly capricious-
ly, touches man with its finger and induces the
impossible exaltation: it can only deal with the effect of
the experience on a very mortal being. Sometimes the
effect seems hardly distinguishable from the highest
secular ecstasy known to us — the sexual one. The
sacramentality of much religious poetry is directly
analogous to the taking of bread and wine at the
ceremony of the eucharist. Whether consecrated or not,
the accidents will taste of bread and wine; the reality is
imposed from without. The analogy to the consecration
in religious poetry is confined to nomenclature — the
name of God or Christ. Sometimes the name is to be
found only in a title or subtitle, as in Hopkins's *The
Windhover — to Christ Our Lord.*

If Hopkins had omitted that dedicatory subtitle, would we regard the sonnet as a religious poem, and, indeed, one of the finest in the language? Probably yes, and not only out of our knowledge that Hopkins was a priest. There is the phrase 'ah my dear', which we know comes straight from George Herbert and, in that exquisite allegory of the divine host and the doubtful guest, still pierces the heart with the directness and intensity of the love it expresses. And there is the ecstasy with which the poet views the kestrel sailing on the wind — an ecstasy too intense to be interpreted as anything smaller than a terrible wonder at the beauty of a creature which implies a greater beauty. Wonder ends in worship.

This anthology, rightly, refuses to limit itself to Christian poetry. There is nothing at all Christian about Wordsworth's *Lines Composed a Few Miles Above Tintern Abbey,* a meditation on the God of Nature which rises to the same sense of wonder as we find in *The Windhover.* The religious ecstasy is genuine, and we do not care whether it is pantheist or Mithraic. But we can see here the peculiar danger which any narrow sectarian (like a Christian Brother in Gibraltar) senses in religious poetry as opposed to mere devotional verse. The religious experience seems to scorn sects and imply a perennial philosophy about grounds of being. To put Wordsworth into a Christian anthology would mean representing him by a few of the ghastly *Ecclesiastical Sonnets.* In Yeats's *The Second Coming,* which is nothing if it is not a religious poem, there is a rough beast slouching to Bethlehem to be born. You can write a genuine religious poem about there being no religion.

Ultimately, I suppose, all literature teaches wonder in the face of a mysterious universe. There is only one poem here by William Shakespeare, and that is about mankind coming to dust, not going to heaven. Will was not good at the expression of faith, and the name Jesus appears only once in his work — in, in fact, that doggerel epitaph which he may well not have written. But no poet or dramatist did better at depicting man lost, bewildered, baffled, looking for meaning, hungering and thirsting after justice. What Shakespeare's work implies is less the existence of God than the need for God to exist. But, throughout his plays and poems, there is a sense of order in the universe, of the unity that lies behind the disparate, of an immense vitality instinct in the world that points to an ineffable source of life. Shakespeare is great because he articulates man's dissatisfactions and needs, but he is not a great religious poet. There is no mysticism in him. He is closer to Montaigne and Seneca than to Donne or Hooker or Herbert. But it is by brooding on what is *not* in Shakespeare that we gain an image of what we would like religious poetry to be — namely, Shakespeare with God in him. We come closest to the realisation of this image in Donne, Herbert and Hopkins. Great religious poetry affirms the world, as Shakespeare does, but it also affirms the Creator of the world. It is not thin, ghostly, scared, conventional. It is more about tigers than about lambs. Its theme, like the poetry of erotism, is human passion, but a passion for, and caused by, ultimate reality.

Anthony Burgess,
Eglise de Sainte-Devote,
Monaco

PLAYING WITH FIRE

From THE BIBLE

c. 10th century B.C.

The Woman
I hear my lover's voice.
He comes running over the mountains,
   racing across the hills to me.
My lover is like a gazelle,
   like a young stag.
There he stands beside the wall.
He looks in through the window
   and glances through the lattice.
My lover speaks to me.

The Man
Come then, my love;
   my darling, come to me.
The winter is over; the rains have stopped;
   in the countryside the flowers are in bloom.
This is the time for singing;
   the song of the doves is heard in the fields.
Figs are beginning to ripen;
   the air is fragrant with blossoming vines.
Come then, my love;
   my darling, come with me.
You are like a dove that hides
   in the crevice of a rock.
Let me see your lovely face
   and hear your enchanting voice.

Song of Songs 2:8-15

ANONYMOUS

7th-12th century

Ireland v Rome

To go to Rome -
   Is little profit, endless pain;
The Master that you seek in Rome,
   You find at home, or seek in vain.

(trans. from the Irish by Frank O'Connor)

O King of the Friday

O King of the Friday
Whose limbs were stretched on the cross,
O Lord who did suffer
The bruises, the wounds, the loss,
We stretch ourselves
Beneath the shield of thy might,
Some fruit from the tree of thy passion
Fall on us this night!

(trans. from the Irish)

ANONYMOUS

7th-12th century

The Priest Rediscovers His Psalm-Book

How good to hear your voice again,
   Old love, no longer young, but true,
As when in Ulster I grew up
   And we were bedmates, I and you.

When first they put us twain to bed,
   My love who speaks the tongue of Heaven,
I was a boy with no bad thoughts,
   A modest youth, and barely seven.

We wandered Ireland over then,
   Our souls and bodies free of blame,
My foolish face aglow with love,
   An idiot without fear of blame.

Yours was the counsel that I sought
   Wherever we went wandering;
Better I found your subtle thought
   Than idle converse with some king.

You slept with four men after that,
   Yet never sinned in leaving me,
And now a virgin you return —
   I say but what all men can see.

For safe within my arms again,
   Weary of wandering many ways,
The face I love is shadowed now
   Though lust attends not its last days.

ANONYMOUS

Faultless my old love seeks me out;
    I welcome her with joyous heart —
My dear, you would not have me lost,
    With you I'll learn that holy art.

Since all the world your praises sings,
    And all acclaim your wanderings past
I have but to heed your counsel sweet
    To find myself with God at last.

You are a token and a sign
    To men of what all men must heed;
Each day your lovers learn anew
    God's praise is all the skill they need.

So may He grant me by your grace
    A quiet end, an easy mind,
And light my pathway with His face
    When the dead flesh is left behind.

(trans. from the Irish by Frank O'Connor)

ANONYMOUS

The Sweetness of Nature

This is one of the songs of the mad king, Suibhne (Sweeney),
from a twelfth-century romance, the material of which goes back
to the eighth century. In this poem Suibhne is flying from the
battlefield, driven mad by the sight of the broken bodies.

Endlessly over the water
    Birds of the Bann are singing;
Sweeter to me their voices
    Than any churchbell's ringing.

Over the plain of Moyra
    Under the heels of foemen
I saw my people broken
    As flax is scutched by women.

But the cries I hear by Derry
    Are not of men triumphant;
I hear their calls in the evening,
    Swans calm and exultant.

I hear the stag's belling
    Over the valley's steepness;
No music on the earth
    Can move me like its sweetness.

Christ, Christ hear me!
    Christ, Christ of Thy meekness!
Christ, Christ love me!
    Sever me not from Thy sweetness!

(trans. from the Irish by Frank O'Connor)

Ascribed to ST PATRICK

8th century

St Patrick's Breastplate

I arise today
Through a mighty strength, the invocation of the
      Trinity,
Through belief in the threeness,
Through confession of the oneness
Of the Creator of Creation.

I arise today
Through the strength of Christ's birth with His baptism,
Through the strength of His crucifixion with His burial,
Through the strength of His resurrection with His
      ascension,
Through the strength of His descent for the judgement of
      Doom.

I arise today
Through the strength of the love of Cherubim,
In obedience of angels,
In the service of archangels,
In hope of resurrection to meet with reward,
In prayers of patriarchs,
In predictions of prophets,
In preaching of apostles,
In faiths of confessors,
In innocence of holy virgins,
In deeds of righteous men.

I arise today
Through the strength of heaven:
Light of sun,

Ascribed to ST PATRICK

Radiance of moon,
Splendour of fire,

Speed of lightning,
Swiftness of wind,
Depth of sea,
Stability of earth,
Firmness of rock.

I arise today
Through God's strength to pilot me:
God's might to uphold me,
God's wisdom to guide me,
God's eye to look before me,
God's ear to hear me,
God's word to speak for me,
God's hand to guard me,
God's way to lie before me,
God's shield to protect me,
God's host to save me
From snares of devils,
From temptations of vices,
From every one who shall wish me ill,
Afar and anear,
Alone and in a multitude.
I summon today all these powers between me and those
      evils,
Against every cruel merciless power that may oppose
      my body and soul,
Against incantations of false prophets,
Against black laws of pagandom,
Against false laws of heretics,
Against craft of idolatry,
Against spells of women and smiths and wizards,
Against every knowledge that corrupts man's body and
      soul.

Christ to shield me today
Against poison, against burning,
Against drowning, against wounding,
So that there may come to me abundance of reward.
Christ with me, Christ before me, Christ behind me,
Christ in me, Christ beneath me, Christ above me,
Christ on my right, Christ on my left,
Christ when I lie down, Christ when I sit down, Christ
    when I arise,
Christ in the heart of every man who thinks of me,
Christ in the mouth of every one who speaks of me,
Christ in every eye that sees me,
Christ in every ear that hears me.

I arise today
Through a mighty strength, the invocation of the Trinity,
Through belief in the threeness,
Through confession of the oneness
Of the Creator of Creation.

(trans. from the Irish by Kuno Meyer)

ANONYMOUS

8th century

 From *The Dream of the Rood*

'It was long years ago — I can recall it yet —
that I was felled   in a place in the forest,
hauled away from my home.   Hostile hands seized me,
bade me lift miscreants up   for men to see their shame.
They heaved me on their shoulders,   set me up upon a
     hill,
crowded round to fix me fast.   Then far off I saw the
     Lord of men
hastening, hero-like   to mount upon me high.
How then could I dare   to disobey my Lord,
to bend or break   even though I beheld
all the earth quaking?   Quick though it would have been
to fell our foes,   I none the less stood fast.
He made ready, the young hero,   he, the Lord of hosts,
resolute and strong   upon his gallows rose aloft,
valiant for the crowd to see,   for he vouchsafed to set
     man free.
I shook as he, the Son of Man, enfolded me,   yet still I
     feared to bow to earth,
fall to the ground: yet still I must stand firm.
I was set up, the Cross,   I lifted up a mighty King,
the heaven's Lord; and yet   I dared not yield.
They stabbed me with their nails of iron black —   my
     wounds can still be seen,
the gaping marks of malice.   Not one of them might I
     harm.
They mocked us both together;   I was suffused with
     blood
poured from the side of the Son of Man   when he had
     sent forth his spirit.'

(E. Colledge)

33

ST FRANCIS OF ASSISI

1182-1226

The Canticle of the Creatures

Most high omnipotent good Lord, to Thee
Praise, glory, honour, and every benediction.

To Thee alone Most High do they belong.
And no man is worthy to pronounce Thy Name.

Praise be to Thee my Lord with all Thy creatures.
Especially for Master Brother Sun
Who illuminates the day for us,
And Thee Most High he manifests.

Praise be to Thee my Lord for Sister Moon and for the
    Stars.
In Heaven Thou hast formed them, shining, precious,
    fair.

Praise be to Thee my Lord for Brother Wind,
For air and clouds, clear sky and all the weathers
Through which Thou sustainest all Thy creatures.

Praise be to Thee my Lord for Sister Water,
She is useful and humble, precious and pure.

Praise be to Thee my Lord for Brother Fire,
Through him our night Thou dost enlighten,
And he is fair and merry, boisterous and strong.

Praise be to Thee my Lord for our sister Mother Earth,
Who nourishes and sustains us all,
Bringing forth divers fruits and many-coloured flowers
    and herbs.

Praise be to Thee my Lord for those who pardon grant
    for love of Thee
And bear infirmity and tribulation,
Blessed be those who live in peace,
For by Thee Most High they shall be crowned.

Praise be to Thee my Lord for our Sister Bodily Death
From whom no living man can flee;
Woe to them who die in mortal sin
But blessed they who shall be found in Thy most holy
    Will;
To them the second death can do no harm.

O bless and praise my Lord all creatures,
And thank and serve Him in deep humility.

ANONYMOUS

14th century

Jesus, my sweet lover

Jesu Christ, my lemmon swete,
That diyedest on the Rode Tree,
With all my might I thee beseche,
For thy woundes two and three,
That also faste mot thy love
Into mine herte fitched be
As was the spere into thine herte,
Whon thou soffredest deth for me.

1. lemmon, *lover.* 5. also, *as,* mot, *may.* 6. fitched, *fixed.*

A Short Prayer to Mary

Blessed Mary, moder virginal,
Integrate maiden, sterre of the see,
Have remembraunce at the day final
On thy poore servaunt now praying to thee.
Mirroure without spot, rede rose of Jerico,
Close garden of grace, hope in disparage,
Whan my soule the body parte fro,
Socoure it from mine enmies' rage.

2. Integrate, *Perfect.* 6. Close, *Closed;* disparage, *despair.*

WILLIAM CORNISH?

Medieval

Pleasure it is

Pleasure it is
To here, iwis,
The birds sing;
The dere in the dale,
The shepe in the vale,
The corne springing.
God's purveaunce
For sustenaunce
It is for man:
Then we always
To give him praise,
And thank him than,
And thank him than.

2. iwis, *indeed.* 7. purveaunce, *provision.*

ANONYMOUS

Medieval

Corpus Christi Carol

Lully, lullay, lully, lullay,
The falcon hath borne my make away.

He bore him up, he bore him down;
He bore him into an orchard brown.

In that orchard there was an hall,
That was hanged with purple and pall.

And in that hall there was a bed
It was hanged with gold so red.

And in that bed there lieth a knight,
His woundes bleeding day and night.

By that bed's side there kneeleth a may,
And she weepeth both night and day.

And by that bed's side there standeth a stone,
Corpus Christi written thereon.

ST JOHN OF THE CROSS

1542-91

Concerning the Divine Word

With the divinest Word, the Virgin
Made pregnant, down the road
Comes walking, if you'll grant her
A room in your abode.

(trans. Roy Campbell)

Upon a gloomy night

Upon a gloomy night,
With all my cares to loving ardours flushed,
(O venture of delight!)
With nobody in sight
I went abroad when all my house was hushed.

In safety, in disguise,
In darkness up the secret stair I crept,
(O happy enterprise)
Concealed from other eyes
When all my house at length in silence slept.

Upon that lucky night
In secrecy, inscrutable to sight,
I went without discerning
And with no other light
Except for that which in my heart was burning.

It lit and led me through
More certain than the light of noonday clear
To where One waited near
Whose presence well I knew,
There where no other presence might appear.

Oh night that was my guide!
Oh darkness dearer than the morning's pride,
Oh night that joined the lover
To the beloved bride
Transfiguring them each into the other.

Within my flowering breast
Which only for himself entire I save
He sank into his rest
And all my gifts I gave
Lulled by the airs with which the cedars wave.

Over the ramparts fanned
While the fresh wind was fluttering his tresses,
With his serenest hand
My neck he wounded, and
Suspended every sense with its caresses.

Lost to myself I stayed
My face upon my lover having laid
From all endeavour ceasing:
And all my cares releasing
Threw them amongst the lilies there to fade.

(trans. Roy Campbell)

SIR PHILIP SIDNEY

1554-86

True Love

My true love hath my heart and I have his,
   By just exchange one for another given;
I hold his dear, and mine he cannot miss,
There never was a better bargain driven.
   My true love hath my heart and I have his.

His heart in me keeps him and me in one,
   My heart in him his thoughts and senses guides;
He loves my heart, for once it was his own,
   I cherish his, because in me it bides.
   My true love hath my heart and I have his.

WILLIAM SHAKESPEARE

1564-1616

From *'Cymbeline,' Act IV*

Fear no more the heat o' the sun,
  Nor the furious winter's rages;
Thou thy worldly task hast done,
  Home art gone, and ta'en thy wages;
Golden lads and girls all must
  As chimney-sweepers, come to dust.

Fear no more the frown o' the great,
  Thou art past the tyrant's stroke:
Care no more to clothe and eat;
  To thee the reed is as the oak;
The sceptre, learning, physic, must
  All follow this, and come to dust.

Fear no more the lightning-flash,
  Nor the all-dreaded thunder-stone;
Fear not slander, censure rash;
  Thou hast finish'd joy and moan:
All lovers young, all lovers must
  Consign to thee, and come to dust.

No exorciser harm thee!
  Nor no witchcraft charm thee!
Ghost unlaid forbear thee!
  Nothing ill come near thee!
Quiet consummation have;
  And renowned be thy grave!

JOHN DONNE

1573-1631

Holy Sonnets III

At the round earth's imagined corners blow
Your trumpets, angels, and arise, arise
From death, you numberless infinities
Of souls, and to your scattered bodies go:
All whom the flood did, and fire shall o'erthrow,
All whom war, dearth, age, agues, tyrannies,
Despair, law, chance hath slain, and you whose eyes
Shall behold God and never taste death's woe.
But let them sleep, Lord, and me mourn a space,
For if above all these my sins abound,
'Tis late to ask abundance of thy grace
When we are there. Here on this lowly ground
Teach me how to repent; for that's as good
As if thou hadst sealed my pardon with thy blood.

JOHN DONNE

Holy Sonnets V

Batter my heart, three-personed God, for you
As yet but knock, breathe, shine, and seek to mend;
That I may rise and stand, o'erthrow me and bend
Your force to break, blow, burn, and make me new.
I, like an usurped town to another due,
Labour to admit you, but O, to no end.
Reason, your viceroy in me, me should defend,
But is captived and proves weak or untrue.

Yet dearly I love you and would be loved fain,
But am betrothed unto your enemy.
Divorce me, untie, or break that knot again,
Take me to you, imprison me, for I,
Except you enthrall me, never shall be free,
Nor ever chaste except you ravish me.

BEN JONSON

1573-1637

A Hymn to God the Father

Hear me, O God!
  A broken heart
  Is my best part:
Use still thy rod
  That I may prove
  Therein thy love.

If thou hadst not
  Been stern to me,
  But let me free,
I had forgot
  Myself and thee.

For sin's so sweet,
  As minds ill bent
  Rarely repent,
Until they meet
  Their punishment.

Who more can crave
  Than thou hast done,
  That gav'st a son
To free a slave,
  First made of nought,
  With all since bought?

Sin, Death, and Hell
  His glorious Name
  Quite overcame,
Yet I rebel,
  And slight the same.

But I'll come in,
Before my loss
Me farther toss,
As sure to win
Under his cross.

To Heaven

Good and great God, can I not think of Thee,
But it must, straight, my melancholy be?
It is interpreted in me disease,
That, laden with my sins I seek for ease?
O, be Thou witness, that the reins dost know
And hearts of all, if I be sad for show,
And judge me after: if I dare pretend
To aught but grace, or aim at other end.
As Thou art all, so be Thou all to me,
First, midst, and last, converted One, and Three;
My Faith, my Hope, my Love: and in this state,
My Judge, my Witness, and my Advocate.
Where have I been this while exiled from Thee?
And whither rapt, now Thou but stoop'st to me?
Dwell, dwell here still: O, being everywhere,
How can I doubt to find Thee ever, here?
I know my state, both full of shame, and scorn,
Conceived in sin, and unto labour born,
Standing with fear, and must with horror fall,
And destined unto judgment, after all.
I feel my griefs too, and there scarce is ground
Upon my flesh to inflict another wound.
Yet dare I not complain, or wish for death
With holy Paul, lest it be thought the breath
Of discontent; or that these prayers be
For weariness of life, not love of Thee.

ROBERT HERRICK

1591-1674

To Keep a True Lent

Is this a Fast, to keep
   The larder lean?
      And clean
From fat of veals and sheep?

Is it to quit the dish
   Of flesh, yet still
      To fill
The platter high with fish?

Is it to fast an hour,
   Or ragg'd to go,
      Or show
A down-cast look and sour?

No: 'tis a Fast to dole
   Thy sheaf of wheat
      And meat
Unto the hungry soul.

It is to fast from strife
   And old debate,
      And hate;
To circumcise thy life.

To show a heart grief-rent;
   To starve thy sin,
      Not bin;
And that's to keep thy Lent.

GEORGE HERBERT

1593-1633

The Call

Come, my Way, my Truth, my Life:
Such a Way, as gives us breath:
Such a Truth, as ends all strife:
Such a Life, as killeth death.

Come, my Light, my Feast, my Strength:
Such a Light, as shows a feast:
Such a Feast, as mends in length:
Such a Strength, as makes his guest.

Come, my Joy, my Love, my Heart:
Such a Joy, as none can move:
Such a Love, as none can part:
Such a Heart, as joys in Love.

GEORGE HERBERT

Love

Love bade me welcome; yet my soul drew back,
    Guilty of dust and sin.
But quick-eyed Love, observing me grow slack
    From my first entrance in,
Drew nearer to me, sweetly questioning,
    If I lacked anything.

'A guest', I answered, 'worthy to be here.'
    Love said, 'You shall be he.'
'I, the unkind, ungrateful? Ah, my dear,
    I cannot look on thee.'
Love took my hand, and smiling did reply,
    'Who made the eyes but I?'

'Truth, Lord, but I have marred them; let my shame
    Go where it doth deserve.'
'And know you not', says Love, 'who bore the blame?'
    'My dear, then I will serve.'
'You must sit down', says Love, 'and taste my meat.'
    So I did sit and eat.

JOHN MILTON

1608-74

On His Blindness

When I consider how my light is spent
Ere half my days, in this dark world and wide,
And that one talent which is death to hide
Lodged with me useless, though my soul more bent

To serve therewith my Maker, and present
My true account, lest He returning chide, —
Doth God exact day-labour, light denied?
I fondly ask: — But Patience, to prevent

That murmur, soon replies; God doth not need
Either man's work, or His own gifts: who best
Bear His mild yoke, they serve Him best: His state

Is kingly; thousands at His bidding speed
And post o'er land and ocean without rest: —
They also serve who only stand and wait.

HENRY VAUGHAN

1622-95

Peace

My soul, there is a country
    Far beyond the stars,
Where stands a winged sentry
    All skilful in the wars:
There above noise and danger
    Sweet Peace sits crowned with smiles,
And One born in a manger
    Commands the beauteous files.
He is thy gracious friend
    And—O my soul, awake!—
Did in pure love descend
    To die here for thy sake.
If thou canst get but thither,
    There grows the flower of Peace,
The Rose that cannot wither,
    Thy fortress, and thy ease.
Leave then thy foolish ranges,
    For none can thee secure,
But one who never changes,
    Thy God, thy life, thy cure.

EDWARD TAYLOR

1645-1729

Huswifery

Make me, O Lord, thy Spining Wheele compleate.
Thy Holy Worde my Distaff make for mee.
Make mine Affections thy Swift Flyers neate
  And make my Soule thy holy Spoole to bee.
  My Conversation make to be thy Reele
  And reele the yarn theron spun of thy Wheele.

Make me thy Loome then, knit therein this Twine:
  And make thy Holy Spirit, Lord, winde quills:
Then weave the Web thyselfe. The yarn is fine.
  Thine Ordinances make my Fulling Mills.
  Then dy the same in Heavenly Colours Choice,
  All pinkt with Varnisht Flowers of Paradise.

Then cloath therewith mine Understanding, Will,
  Affections, Judgment, Conscience, Memory
My Words, and Actions, that their shine may fill
  My wayes with glory and thee glorify.
  Then mine apparell shall display before yee
  That I am Cloathd in Holy robes for glory.

WILLIAM BLAKE

1757-1827

The Tyger

Tyger! Tyger! burning bright
In the forests of the night,
What immortal hand or eye
Could frame thy fearful symmetry?

In what distant deeps or skies
Burnt the fire of thine eyes?
On what wings dare he aspire?
What the hand dare sieze the fire?

And what shoulder, & what art,
Could twist the sinews of thy heart?
And when thy heart began to beat,
What dread hand? & what dread feet?

What the hammer? what the chain?
In what furnace was thy brain?
What the anvil? what dread grasp
Dare its deadly terrors clasp?

When the stars threw down their spears,
And water'd heaven with their tears,
Did he smile his work to see?
Did he who made the Lamb make thee?

Tyger! Tyger! burning bright
In the forests of the night,
What immortal hand or eye
Dare frame thy fearful symmetry?

WILLIAM BLAKE

The Divine Image

To Mercy, Pity, Peace, and Love
All pray in their distress;
And to these virtues of delight,
Return their thankfulness.

For Mercy, Pity, Peace, and Love
Is God, our father dear,
And Mercy, Pity, Peace, and Love
Is man, his child and care.

For Mercy has a human heart,
Pity a human face,
And Love, the human form divine,
And Peace, the human dress.

Then every man, of every clime,
That prays in his distress,
Prays to the human form divine,
Love, Mercy, Pity, Peace.

And all must love the human form,
In heathen, turk, or jew;
Where Mercy, Love, and Pity dwell
There God is dwelling too.

WILLIAM BLAKE

A Divine Image

Cruelty has a Human Heart,
And Jealousy a Human Face;
Terror the Human Form Divine,
And Secrecy the Human Dress.

The Human Dress is forged Iron,
The Human Form a fiery Forge,
The Human Face a Furnace seal'd,
The Human Heart its hungry Gorge.

WILLIAM BLAKE

Holy Thursday

'Twas on a Holy Thursday, their innocent faces clean,
The children walking two & two, in red & blue & green,
Grey-headed beadles walk'd before, with wands as white
            as snow,
Till into the high dome of Paul's they like Thames'
            waters flow.

O what a multitude they seem'd, these flowers of London
            town!
Seated in companies they sit with radiance all their own.
The hum of multitudes was there, but multitudes of
            lambs,
Thousands of little boys & girls raising their innocent
            hands.

Now like a mighty wind they raise to heaven the voice of
            song,
Or like harmonious thunderings the seats of heaven
            among.
Beneath them sit the aged men, wise guardians of the
            poor;
Then cherish pity, lest you drive an angel from your
            door.

Holy Thursday

Is this a holy thing to see
In a rich and fruitful land,
Babes reduc'd to misery,
Fed with cold and usurous hand?

Is that trembling cry a song?
Can it be a song of joy?
And so many children poor?
It is a land of poverty!

And their sun does never shine,
And their fields are black & bare,
And their ways are fill'd with thorns:
It is eternal winter there.

For where-e'er the sun does shine,
And where-e'er the rain does fall,
Babe can never hunger there,
Nor poverty the mind appall.

WILLIAM WORDSWORTH

1770-1850

Lines Composed a Few Miles Above Tintern Abbey

                       The sounding cataract
Haunted me like a passion; the tall rock,
The mountain, and the deep and gloomy wood,
Their colours and their forms, were then to me
An appetite; a feeling and a love,
That had no need of a remoter charm,
By thought supplied, nor any interest
Unborrowed from the eye. — That time is past.
And all its aching joys are now no more,
And all its dizzy raptures. Not for this
Faint I, nor mourn, nor murmur; other gifts
Have followed; for such loss, I would believe,
Abundant recompense. For I have learned
To look on Nature, not as in the hour
Of thoughtless youth; but hearing oftentimes
The still, sad music of humanity,
Nor harsh, nor grating, though of ample power
To chasten and subdue. And I have felt
A presence that disturbs me with the joy
Of elevated thoughts; a sense sublime,
Of something far more deeply interfused,
Whose dwelling is the light of setting suns,
And the round ocean and the living air,
And the blue sky, and in the mind of man;
A motion and a spirit, that impels
All thinking things, all objects of all thought,
And rolls through all things. Therefore am I still
A lover of the meadows and the woods,
And mountains; and of all that we behold
From this green earth; of all the mighty world

Of eye and ear, — both what they half create,
And what perceive; well pleased to recognize
In nature and the language of the sense,
The anchor of my purest thoughts, the nurse,
The guide, the guardian of my heart, and soul
Of all my moral being.

J. H. NEWMAN

1801-90

From *The Dream of Gerontius*

Pray for me, O my friends; a visitant
    Is knocking his dire summons at my door,
The like of whom, to scare me and to daunt,
    Has never, never come to me before;
'Tis death — O loving friends, your prayers! — 'tis he! . . .
As though my very being had given way,
    As though I was no more a substance now,
And could fall back on nought to be my stay,
    (Help, loving lord! Thou my sole Refuge, Thou,)
And turn no whither, but must needs decay
    And drop from out the universal frame
Into that shapeless, scopeless, blank abyss,
    That utter nothingness, of which I came:
This is it that has come to pass in me;
O horror! this is it, my dearest, this;
So pray for me, my friends, who have not strength to pray.

EDGAR ALLAN POE

1809-49

A Dream within a Dream

Take this kiss upon the brow!
And, in parting from you now,
Thus much let me avow —
You are not wrong, who deem
That my days have been a dream;
Yet if Hope has flown away
In a night, or in a day,
In a vision, or in none,
Is it therefore the less *gone*?
All that we see or seem
Is but a dream within a dream.

I stand amid the roar
Of a surf-tormented shore,
And I hold within my hand
Grains of the golden sand —
How few! yet how they creep
Through my fingers to the deep,
While I weep — while I weep!
Oh God! can I not grasp
Them with a tighter clasp?
O God! can I not save
One from the pitiless wave?
Is *all* that we see or seem
But a dream within a dream?

ALFRED TENNYSON

1809-92

The Shell

See what a lovely shell,
Small and pure as a pearl,
Lying close to my foot,
Frail, but a work divine,
Made so fairly well
With delicate spire and whorl.
How exquisitely minute,
A miracle of design.

What is it? a learned man
Could give it a clumsy name.
Let him name it who can,
The beauty would be the same.

The tiny cell is forlorn,
Void of the little living will
That made it stir on the shore.
Did he stand at the diamond door
Of his house in a rainbow frill?
Did he push when he was uncurled
A golden foot or a fairy horn
Through his dim water world?

Slight, to be crushed with a tap
Of my finger-nail on the sand,
Small, but a work divine,
Frail, but of force to withstand,
Year upon year, the shock
Of cataract seas that snap
The three-decker's oaken spine
Athwart the ledges of rock
Here on the Breton strand!

HENRY DAVID THOREAU

1817-62

Great God, I ask Thee for No Meaner Pelf

Great God, I ask thee for no meaner pelf
Than that I may not disappoint myself,
That in my action I may soar as high,
As I can now discern with this clear eye.

And next in value, which thy kindness lends,
That I may greatly disappoint my friends,
Howe'er they think or hope that it may be,
They may not dream how thou'st distinguished me.

That my weak hand may equal my firm faith,
And my life practice more than my tongue saith;
That my low conduct may not show,
Nor my relenting lines,
That I thy purpose did not know,
Or overrated thy designs.

Light-Winged Smoke, Icarian Bird

Light-winged Smoke, Icarian bird,
Melting thy pinions in thy upward flight,
Lark without song, and messenger of dawn,
Circling above the hamlets as thy nest;
Or else, departing dream, and shadowy form
Of midnight vision, gathering up thy skirts;
By night star-veiling, and by day
Darkening the light and blotting out the sun;
Go thou my incense upward from this hearth,
And ask the gods to pardon this clear flame.

WALT WHITMAN

1819-92

Miracles

As to me I know nothing else but miracles,
Whether I walk the streets of Manhatten,
Or dart my sight over the roofs of houses toward the
    sky,
Or wade with naked feet along the beach just in the
    edge of the water,
Or stand under trees in the woods,
Or talk by day with any one I love,
Or sit at table at dinner with the rest,
Or look at strangers opposite me riding in the car,
Or watch honey bees busy around the hive of a summer
    forenoon,
Or animals feeding in the fields,
Or birds, or the wonderfulness of insects in the air,
Or the wonderfulness of the sundown, or of stars
    shining so quiet and bright,
Or the exquisite delicate thin curve of the new moon
    in spring;
These with the rest, one and all, are to me miracles.

EMILY DICKINSON

1830-86

My life closed twice before its close

My life closed twice before its close —
It yet remains to see
If Immortality unveil
A third event to me

So huge, so hopeless to conceive
As these that twice befell.
Parting is all we know of heaven,
And all we need of hell.

God is indeed a jealous God

God is indeed a jealous God —
He cannot bear to see
That we had rather not with Him
But with each other play.

EMILY DICKINSON

This world is not conclusion

This world is not Conclusion.
A Species stands beyond —
Invisible, as Music —
But positive, as Sound —
It beckons, and it baffles —
Philosophy — don't know —
And through a Riddle, at the last —
Sagacity, must go —
To guess it, puzzles scholars —
To gain it, Men have borne
Contempt of Generations
And Crucifixion, shown —
Faith slips — and laughs, and rallies —
Blushes, if any see —
Plucks at a twig of Evidence —
And asks a Vane, the way —
Much Gesture, from the Pulpit —
Strong Hallelujahs roll —
Narcotics cannot still the Tooth
That nibbles at the soul —

THOMAS HARDY

1840-1928

Afternoon Service at Mellstock
(circa 1850)

On afternoons of drowsy calm
We stood in the panelled pew,
Singing one-voiced a Tate-and-Brady psalm
To the tune of 'Cambridge New.'

We watched the elms, we watched the rooks,
The clouds upon the breeze,
Between the whiles of glancing at our books,
And swaying like the trees.

So mindless were those outpourings! —
Though I am not aware
That I have gained by subtle thought on things
Since we stood psalming there.

THOMAS HARDY

The Darkling Thrush

I leant upon a coppice gate
    When Frost was spectre-gray,
And Winter's dregs made desolate
    The weakening eye of day.
The tangled bine-stems scored the sky
    Like strings of broken lyres,
And all mankind that haunted nigh
    Had sought their household fires.

The land's sharp features seemed to be
    The Century's corpse outleant,
His crypt the cloudy canopy,
    The wind his death-lament.
The ancient pulse of germ and birth
    Was shrunken hard and dry,
And every spirit upon earth
    Seemed fervourless as I.

At once a voice arose among
    The bleak twigs overhead
In a full-hearted evensong
    Of joy illimited;
An aged thrush, frail, gaunt, and small,
    In blast-beruffled plume,
Had chosen thus to fling his soul
    Upon the growing gloom.

So little cause for carolings
    Of such ecstatic sound
Was written on terrestrial things
    Afar or nigh around,
That I could think there trembled through
    His happy good-night air
Some blessed Hope, whereof he knew
    And I was unaware.
           31st December 1900

THOMAS HARDY

In Church

'And now to God the Father,' he ends,
And his voice thrills up to the topmost tiles:
Each listener chokes as he bows and bends,
And emotion pervades the crowded aisles.
Then the preacher glides to the vestry-door,
And shuts it, and thinks he is seen no more.

The door swings softly ajar meanwhile,
And a pupil of his in the Bible class,
Who adores him as one without gloss or guile,
Sees her idol stand with a satisfied smile
And re-enact at the vestry-glass
Each pulpit gesture in deft dumb-show
That had moved the congregation so.

SIDNEY LANIER

1842-81

A Ballad of Trees and the Master

Into the woods my Master went,
  Clean forspent, forspent.
Into the woods my Master came,
  Forspent with love and shame.
But the olives they were not blind to Him,
The little gray leaves were kind to Him:
The thorn-tree had a mind to Him
  When into the wood He came.

Out of the woods my Master went,
  And He was well content.
Out of the woods my Master came,
  Content with death and shame.
When Death and Shame would woo Him last,
From under the trees they drew Him last:
'Twas on a tree they slew Him — last
  When out of the woods He came.

GERARD MANLEY HOPKINS

1844-89

The Windhover
To Christ our Lord

I caught this morning morning's minion, king-
   dom of daylight's dauphin, dapple-dawn-drawn
     Falcon, in his riding
   Of the rolling level underneath him steady air, and
     striding
High there, how he rung upon the rein of a wimpling
     wing
In his ecstasy! then off, off forth on swing,
   As a skate's heel sweeps smooth on a bow-bend: the
     hurl and gliding
Rebuffed the big wind. My heart in hiding
Stirred for a bird,—the achieve of, the mastery of the
     thing!

Brute beauty and valour and act, oh, air, pride, plume,
     here
   Buckle! AND the fire that breaks from thee then, a
     billion
Times told lovelier, more dangerous, O my chevalier!

   No wonder of it: shéer plód makes plough down
     sillion
Shine, and blue-bleak embers, ah my dear,
   Fall, gall themselves, and gash gold-vermilion.

That Nature is a Heraclitean Fire and of the Comfort of the Resurrection

Cloud-puffball, torn tufts, tossed pillows |
    flaunt forth, then chevy on an air-
built thoroughfare: heaven-roysterers, in gay-gangs |
    they throng: they glitter in marches.
Down roughcast, down dazzling whitewash, | wher-
    ever an elm arches,
Shivelights and shadowtackle in long | lashes lace, lance,
    and pair.
Delightfully the bright wind boisterous | ropes,
    wrestles, beats earth bare
Of yestertempest's creases; in pool and rut peel parches
Squandering ooze to squeezed | dough, crust, dust;
    stanches, starches
Squadroned masks and manmarks | treadmire toil there
Footfretted in it. Million-fuelèd, | nature's bonfire
    burns on.
But quench her bonniest, dearest | to her, her clearest-
    selvèd spark
Man, how fast his firedint, | his mark on mind, is gone!
Both are in an unfathomable, all is in an enormous dark
Drowned. O pity and indig | nation! Manshape, that
    shone
Sheer off, disseveral, a star, | death blots black out;
    nor mark
        Is any of him at all so stark
But vastness blurs and time | beats level. Enough! the
    Resurrection,
A heart's-clarion! Away grief's gasping, | joyless days,
    dejection.

> Across my foundering deck shone
A beacon, an eternal beam. | Flesh fade, and mortal trash
Fall to the residuary worm; world's wildfire, leave but
> ash:
> In a flash, at a trumpet crash,
I am all at once what Christ is, | since he was what I am,
> and
This Jack, joke, poor potsherd, | patch, matchwood,
> immortal diamond,
> Is immortal diamond.

A. E. HOUSMAN

1859-1936

Oh Who is that Young Sinner

Oh who is that young sinner with the handcuffs on
    his wrists?
And what has he been after that they groan and shake
    their fists?
And wherefore is he wearing such a conscience-stricken
    air?
Oh they're taking him to prison for the colour of his
    hair.

'Tis a shame to human nature, such a head of hair as
    his;
In the good old time 'twas hanging for the colour that
    it is;
Though hanging isn't bad enough and flaying would
    be fair
For the nameless and abominable colour of his hair.

Oh a deal of pains he's taken and a pretty price he's paid
To hide his poll or dye it of a mentionable shade;
But they've pulled the beggar's hat off for the world
    to see and stare,
And they're taking him to justice for the colour of his
    hair.

Now 'tis oakum for his fingers and the treadmill for
    his feet,
And the quarry-gang of Portland in the cold and in
    the heat,
And between his spells of labour in the time he has to
    spare
He can curse the God that made him for the colour of
    his hair.

FREDERICK GEORGE SCOTT

1861-1944

The Sting of Death

'Is Sin, then, fair?'
   Nay, love, come now,
Put back the hair
   From his sunny brow;
See, here, blood-red
   Across his head
A brand is set,
The word — 'Regret.'

'Is Sin so fleet
   That while he stays,
Our hands and feet
   May go his ways?'
Nay, love, his breath
Clings round like death,
He slakes desire
With liquid fire.

'Is Sin Death's sting?'
   Ay, sure he is,
His golden wing
   Darkens man's bliss;
And when Death comes,
Sin sits and hums
A chaunt of fears
Into man's ears.

FREDERICK GEORGE SCOTT

'How slayeth Sin?'
　　First, God is hid,
And the heart within
　　By its own self chid;
Then the maddened brain
Is scourged by pain
To sin as before
And more and more,
　　For evermore.

RABINDRANATH TAGORE

1861-1941

Leave this chanting and singing and telling of beads!

Leave this chanting and singing and telling of beads!
Whom dost thou worship in this lonely dark corner of a
temple with doors all shut? Open thine eyes and see thy
God is not before thee!

He is there where the tiller is tilling the hard ground and
where the pathmaker is breaking stones. He is with them
in sun and in shower, and his garment is covered with
dust. Put off thy holy mantle and even like him come
down on the dusty soil!

Deliverance? Where is this deliverance to be found? Our
master himself has joyfully taken upon him the bonds
of creation; he is bound with us all for ever.

Come out of thy meditations and leave aside thy flowers
and incense! What harm is there if thy clothes become
tattered and stained? Meet him and stand by him in toil
and in sweat of thy brow.

W. B. YEATS

1865-1939

An Irish Airman Foresees his Death

I know that I shall meet my fate
Somewhere among the clouds above;
Those that I fight I do not hate,
Those that I guard I do not love;
My country is Kiltartan Cross,
My countrymen Kiltartan's poor,
No likely end could bring them loss
Or leave them happier than before.
Nor law, nor duty bade me fight,
Nor public men, nor cheering crowds,
A lonely impulse of delight
Drove to this tumult in the clouds.
I balanced all, brought all to mind,
The years to come seemed waste of breath,
A waste of breath the years behind
In balance with this life, this death.

The Mother of God

The threefold terror of love; a fallen flare
Through the hollow of an ear;
Wings beating about the room;
The terror of all terrors that I bore
The Heavens in my womb.

Had I not found content among the shows
Every common woman knows,
Chimney corner, garden walk,
Or rocky cistern where we tread the clothes
And gather all the talk?

What is this flesh I purchased with my pains
This fallen star my milk sustains,
This love that makes my heart's blood stop
Or strikes a sudden chill into my bones
And bids my hair stand up?

The Second Coming

Turning and turning in the widening gyre
The falcon cannot hear the falconer;
Things fall apart; the centre cannot hold;
Mere anarchy is loosed upon the world,
The blood-dimmed tide is loosed, and everywhere
The ceremony of innocence is drowned;
The best lack all conviction, while the worst
Are full of passionate intensity.

Surely some revelation is at hand;
Surely the Second Coming is at hand.
The Second Coming! Hardly are those words out
When a vast image out of *Spiritus Mundi*
Troubles my sight: somewhere in sands of the desert
A shape with lion body and the head of a man.
A gaze blank and pitiless as the sun,
Is moving its slow thighs, while all about it
Reel shadows of the indignant desert birds.
The darkness drops again; but now I know
That twenty centuries of stony sleep
Were vexed to nightmare by a rocking cradle,
And what rough beast, its hour come round at last,
Slouches towards Bethlehem to be born?

HILAIRE BELLOC

1870-1953

Upon God the Wine-Giver
(for Easter Sunday)

Though Man made wine, I think God made it too;
God, making all things, made Man make good wine.
He taught him how the little tendrils twine
About the stakes of labour close and true.
Then next, with intimate prophetic laughter,
He taught the Man, in His own image blest,
To pluck and waggon and to — all the rest!
To tread the grape and work his vintage after.

So did God make us, making good wine's makers;
So did he order us to rule the field.
And now by God are we not only bakers
But vintners also, sacraments to yield;
Yet most of all strong lovers. Praise be God!
Who taught us how the wine-press should be trod.

Ballade of Illegal Ornaments

'. . . the controversy was ended by His Lordship, who wrote to the Incumbent ordering him to remove from the Church all Illegal Ornaments at once, and especially a Female Figure with a Child'

I

When that the Eternal deigned to look
   On us poor folk to make us free,
He chose a Maiden, whom He took
   From Nazareth in Galilee;
   Since when the Islands of the Sea,
The Field, the City, and the Wild
   Proclaim aloud triumphantly
A Female Figure with a Child.

II

These Mysteries profoundly shook
   The Reverend Doctor Leigh, D.D.,
Who therefore stuck into a Nook
   (or Niche) of his Incumbency
   An Image filled with majesty
To represent the Undefiled,
   The Universal Mother — She —
A Female Figure with a Child.

III

His Bishop, having read a book
   Which proved as plain as plain could be
That all the Mutts had been mistook
   Who talked about a Trinity,

Wrote off at once to Doctor Leigh
In manner very far from mild,
    And said: "Remove them instantly!
A Female Figure with a Child!"

Envoi

Prince Jesus, in mine Agony,
    Permit me, broken and defiled,
Through blurred and glazing eyes to see
    A Female Figure with a Child.

G. K. CHESTERTON

1874-1936

The Donkey

When fishes flew and forests walked
 And figs grew upon thorn,
Some moment when the moon was blood
 Then surely I was born.

With monstrous head and sickening cry
 And ears like errant wings,
The devil's walking parody
 Of all four-footed things.

The tattered outlaw of the earth,
 Of ancient crooked will;
Starve, scourge, deride me: I am dumb,
 I keep my secret still.

Fools! For I also had my hour;
 One far fierce hour and sweet;
There was a shout about my ears,
 And palms before my feet.

RAINER MARIA RILKE

1875-1926

You, Neighbour God

You, neighbour God, if sometimes in the night
I rouse you with loud knocking, I do so
only because I seldom hear you breathe;
I know: you are alone.
And should you need a drink, no one is there
to reach it to you, groping in the dark.
Always I hearken. Give but a small sign.
I am quite near.

Between us there is but a narrow wall,
and by sheer chance; for it would take
merely a call from your lips or from mine
to break it down,
and that without a sound.

The wall is builded of your images.

They stand before you hiding you like names,
And when the light within me blazes high
that in my inmost soul I know you by,
the radiance is squandered on their frames.

And then my senses, which too soon grow lame,
exiled from you, must go their homeless ways.

JOHN MASEFIELD

1878-1967

O Christ who holds the open gate

O Christ who holds the open gate,
O Christ who drives the furrow straight,
O Christ, the plough, O Christ, the laughter,
Of holy white birds flying after,
Lo, all my heart's field red and torn,
And thou wilt bring the young green corn
The young green corn divinely springing,
The young green corn for ever singing;
And when the field is fresh and fair
Thy blessed feet shall glitter there,
And we will walk the weeded field
And tell the golden harvest's yield,
The corn that makes the holy bread
By which the soul of man is fed,
The holy bread, the food unpriced,
The everlasting mercy, Christ.

D. H. LAWRENCE

1885-1930

Phoenix

Are you willing to be sponged out, erased, cancelled,
  made nothing?
Are you willing to be made nothing?
dipped into oblivion?
If not, you will never really change.

The phoenix renews her youth
only when she is burnt, burnt alive, burnt down
to hot and flocculent ash.
Then the small stirring of a new small bub in the nest
with strands of down like floating ash
Shows that she is renewing her youth like the eagle,
Immortal bird.

Pax

All that matters is to be at one with the living God
to be a creature in the house of the God of Life.

Like a cat asleep on a chair
at peace, in peace
and at one with the master of the house, with the
    mistress,
at home, at home in the house of the living,
sleeping on the hearth, and yawning before the fire.

Sleeping on the hearth of the living world,
yawning at home before the fire of life
feeling the presence of the living God
like a great reassurance
a deep calm in the heart
a presence
as of a master sitting at the board
in his own and greater-being,
in the house of life.

HILDA DOOLITTLE

1886-1961

The Mysteries Remain

The mysteries remain,
I keep the same
cycle of seed-time
and of sun and rain;
Demeter in the grass,
I multiply,
renew and bless
Iacchus in the vine;
I hold the law,
I keep the mysteries true,
the first of these
to name the living, dead;
I am red wine and bread.

> *I keep the law,*
> *I hold the mysteries true,*
> *I am the vine,*
> *the branches, you*
> *and you.*

SIEGFRIED SASSOON

1886-1967

Stand to: Good Friday Morning

I'd been on duty from two till four.
I went and stared at the dug-out door.
Down in the frowst I heard them snore.
'Stand to!' Somebody grunted and swore.
   Dawn was misty; the skies were still;
   Larks were singing, discordant, shrill;
   They seemed happy; but I felt ill.
Deep in water I splashed my way
Up the trench to our bogged front line.
Rain had fallen the whole damned night.
O Jesus, send me a wound today,
And I'll believe in Your bread and wine,
And get my bloody old sins washed white!

MARIANNE MOORE

1887-1972

What Are Years?

What is our innocence,
what is our guilt? All are
    naked, none is safe. And whence
is courage: the unanswered question,
the resolute doubt —
dumbly calling, deafly listening — that
is misfortune, even death,
    encourages others
    and in its defeat, stirs

    the soul to be strong? He
sees deep and glad, who
    accedes to mortality
and in his imprisonment rises
upon himself as
the sea in a chasm, struggling to be
free and unable to be,
    in its surrendering
    finds its continuing.

    So he who strongly feels,
behaves. The very bird,
    grown taller as he sings, steels
his form straight up. Though he is captive,
his mighty singing
says, satisfaction is a lowly
thing, how pure a thing is joy.
    This is mortality,
    this is eternity.

EDWIN MUIR

1887-1959

In Love For Long

I've been in love for long
With what I cannot tell
And will contrive a song
For the intangible
That has no mould or shape,
From which there's no escape.

It is not even a name,
Yet is all constancy;
Tried or untried, the same,
It cannot part from me;
A breath, yet as still
As the established hill.

It is not any thing,
And yet all being is;
Being, being, being,
Its burden and its bliss.
How can I ever prove
What it is I love?

This happy happy love
Is sieged with crying sorrows,
Crushed beneath and above
Between todays and morrows;
A little paradise
Held in the world's vice.

And there it is content
And careless as a child,

And in imprisonment
Flourishes sweet and wild;
In wrong, beyond wrong,
All the world's day long.

This love a moment known
For what I do not know
And in a moment gone
Is like the happy doe
That keeps its perfect laws
Between the tiger's paws
And vindicates its cause.

The Killing

That was the day they killed the Son of God
On a squat hill-top by Jerusalem.
Zion was bare, her children from their maze
Sucked by the demon curiosity
Clean through the gates. The very halt and blind
Had somehow got themselves up to the hill.

After the ceremonial preparation,
The scourging, nailing, nailing against the wood,
Erection of the main-trees with their burden,
While from the hill rose an orchestral wailing,
They were there at last, high up in the soft spring day.
We watched the writhings, heard the moanings, saw
The three heads turning on their separate axles
Like broken wheels left spinning. Round his head
Was loosely bound a crown of plaited thorn
That hurt at random, stinging temple and brow
As the pain swung into its envious circle.
In front the wreath was gathered in a knot
That as he gazed looked like the last stump left

Of a death-wounded deer's great antlers. Some
Who came to stare grew silent as they looked,
Indignant or sorry. But the hardened old
And the hard-hearted young, although at odds
From the first morning, cursed him with one curse,
Having prayed for a Rabbi or an armed Messiah
And found the Son of God. What use to them
Was a God or a Son of God? Of what avail
For purposes such as theirs? Beside the cross-foot
Alone, four women stood and did not move
All day. The sun revolved, the shadow wheeled,
The evening fell. His head lay on his breast,
But in his breast they watched his heart move on
By itself alone, accomplishing its journey.
Their taunts grew louder, sharpened by the knowledge
That he was walking in the park of death,
Far from their rage. Yet all grew stale at last,
Spite, curiosity, envy, hate itself.
They waited only for death and death was slow
And came so quietly they scarce could mark it.
They were angry then with death and death's deceit.

I was a stranger, could not read these people
Or this outlandish deity. Did a God
Indeed in dying cross my life that day
By chance, he on his road and I on mine?

JOSEPH PLUNKETT

1887-1916

I See His Blood Upon the Rose

I see his blood upon the rose
And in the stars the glory of his eyes,
His body gleams amid eternal snows,
His tears fall from the skies.

I see his face in every flower;
The thunder and the singing of the birds
Are but his voice — and carven by his power
Rocks are his written words.

All pathways by his feet are worn,
His strong heart stirs the ever-beating sea,
His crown of thorns is twined with every thorn,
His cross is every tree.

EDITH SITWELL

1887-1964

Still Falls the Rain
The Raids, 1940. Night and Dawn

Still falls the Rain —
Dark as the world of man, black as our loss —
Blind as the nineteen hundred and forty nails
Upon the Cross.

Still falls the Rain
With a sound like the pulse of the heart that is changed
    to the hammer-beat
In the Potter's Field, and the sound of the impious feet

On the Tomb:
        Still falls the Rain
In the Field of Blood where the small hopes breed and
    the human brain
Nurtures its greed, that worm with the brow of Cain.

Still falls the Rain
At the feet of the Starved Man hung upon the Cross.
Christ that each day, each night, nails there, have mercy
    on us—
On Dives and on Lazarus:
Under the Rain the sore and the gold are as one.

Still falls the Rain—
Still falls the Blood from the Starved Man's wounded
    Side:
He bears in His Heart all wounds,—those of the light
    that died,
The last faint spark

In the self-murdered heart, the wounds of the sad
        uncomprehending dark,
The wounds of the baited bear,—
The blind and weeping bear whom the keepers beat
On his helpless flesh . . . the tears of the hunted hare.

Still falls the Rain—
Then—O Ile leape up to my God: who pulles me doune—
See, see where Christ's blood streames in the firmament:
It flows from the Brow we nailed upon the tree
Deep to the dying, to the thirsting heart
That holds the fires of the world,—dark-smirched with
        pain
As Caesar's laurel crown.

Then sounds the voice of One who like the heart of man
Was once a child who among beasts has lain—
'Still do I love, still shed my innocent light, my Blood,
        for thee.'

T. S. ELIOT

1888-1965

The Cultivation of Christmas Trees

There are several attitudes towards Christmas
Some of which we may disregard:
The social, the torpid, the patently commercial,
The rowdy (the pubs being open till midnight),
And the childish — which is not that of the child
For whom the candle is a star, and the gilded angel
Spreading its wings at the summit of the tree
Is not only a decoration, but an angel.
The child wonders at the Christmas Tree:
Let him continue in the spirit of wonder
At the Feast as an event not accepted as a pretext:
So that the glittering rapture, the amazement
Of the first-remembered Christmas Tree,
So that the surprises, delight in new possessions
(Each one with its peculiar and exciting smell),
The expectation of the goose or turkey
And the expected awe on its appearance,
So that the reverence and the gaiety
May not be forgotten in later experience,
In the bored habituation, the fatigue, the tedium,
The awareness of death, the consciousness of failure,
Or in the piety of the convert
Which may be tainted with a self-conceit
Displeasing to God and disrespectful to the children
(And here I remember also with gratitude
St Lucy, her carol, and her crown of fire):
So that before the end, the eightieth Christmas
(By 'eightieth' meaning whichever is the last)
The accumulated memories of annual emotion
May be concentrated into a great joy

Which shall be also a great fear, as on the occasion
When fear came upon every soul:
Because the beginning shall remind us of the end
And the first coming of the second coming.

Journey of the Magi

'A cold coming we had of it,
Just the worst time of the year
For a journey, and such a long journey:
The ways deep and the weather sharp,
The very dead of winter.'
And the camels galled, sore-footed, refractory,
Lying down in the melting snow.
There were times we regretted
The summer palaces on slopes, the terraces,
And the silken girls bringing sherbet.
Then the camel men cursing and grumbling
And running away, and wanting their liquor and women,
And the night-fires going out, and the lack of shelters,
And the cities hostile and the towns unfriendly
And the villages dirty and charging high prices:
A hard time we had of it.
At the end we preferred to travel all night,
Sleeping in snatches,
With the voices singing in our ears, saying
That this was all folly.

Then at dawn we came down to a temperate valley,
Wet, below the snow line, smelling of vegetation,
With a running stream and a water-mill beating the
          darkness,
And three trees on the low sky.
And an old white horse galloped away in the meadow.
Then we came to a tavern with vine-leaves over the lintel,

Six hands at an open door dicing for pieces of silver,
And feet kicking the empty wine-skins.
But there was no information, so we continued
And arrived at evening, not a moment too soon
Finding the place; it was (you may say) satisfactory.
All this was a long time ago, I remember,
And I would do it again, but set down
This set down
This: were we led all that way for
Birth or Death? There was a Birth, certainly,
We had evidence and no doubt. I had seen birth and
            death,
But had thought they were different; this Birth was
Hard and bitter agony for us, like Death, our death.
We returned to our places, these Kingdoms,
But no longer at ease here, in the old dispensation,
With an alien people clutching their gods.
I should be glad of another death.'

WILFRED OWEN

1893-1918

At a Calvary near the Ancre

One ever hangs where shelled roads part.
  In this war He too lost a limb,
But His disciples hide apart;
  And now the Soldiers bear with Him.

Near Golgotha strolls many a priest,
  And in their faces there is pride
That they were flesh-marked by the Beast
  By whom the gentle Christ's denied.

The scribes on all the people shove
  And brawl allegiance to the state,
But they who love the greater love
  Lay down their life; they do not hate.

The Parable of the Old Man and the Young

So Abram rose, and clave the wood, and went,
And took the fire with him, and a knife.
And as they sojourned both of them together,
Isaac the first-born spake and said, My Father,
Behold the preparations, fire and iron,
But where the lamb for this burnt-offering?
Then Abram bound the youth with belts and straps,
And builded parapets and trenches there,
And stretchèd forth the knife to slay his son.
When lo! an angel called him out of heaven,
Saying, Lay not thy hand upon the lad,
Neither do anything to him. Behold,
A ram, caught in a thicket by its horns;
Offer the Ram of Pride instead of him.
But the old man would not so, but slew his son,
And half the seed of Europe, one by one.

E. E. CUMMINGS

1894-1962

i thank you God for most this amazing

i thank You God for most this amazing
day: for the leaping greenly spirits of trees
and a blue true dream of sky; and for everything
which is natural which is infinite which is yes

(i who have died am alive again today,
and this is the sun's birthday; this is the birth
day of life and of love and wings: and of the gay
great happening illimitably earth)

how should tasting touching hearing seeing
breathing any — lifted from the no
of all nothing — human merely being
doubt unimaginable You?

(now the ears of my ears awake and
now the eyes of my eyes are opened)

Jehovah buried, Satan dead

Jehovah buried, Satan dead,
do fearers worship Much and Quick;
badness not being felt as bad,
itself thinks goodness what is meek;
obey says too, submit says tic,
Eternity's a Five Year Plan:
if Joy with Pain shall hang in hock
who dares to call himself a man?

go dreamless knaves on Shadows fed,
your Harry's Tom, your Tom is Dick;
while Gadgets murder squawk and add,
the cult of Same is all the chic;
by instruments, both span and spic,
are justly measured Spic and Span:
to kiss the mike if Jew turn kike
who dares to call himself a man?

loudly for Truth have liars pled,
their heels for Freedom slaves will click;
where Boobs are holy, poets mad,
illustrious punks of Progress shriek;
when Souls are outlawed, Hearts are sick,
Hearts being sick, Minds nothing can:
if Hate's a game and Love's a fuck
who dares to call himself a man?

King Christ, this world is all aleak;
and lifepreservers there are none:
and waves which only He may walk
Who dares to call Himself a man.

DAVID JONES

1895-1974

A,a,a Domine Deus, c. 1938 and 1966

I said, Ah! what shall I write?
I enquired up and down.
    (He's tricked me before
with his manifold lurking-places.)
I looked for His symbol at the door.
I have looked for a long while
    at the textures and contours.
I have run a hand over the trivial intersections.
I have journeyed among the dead forms
    causation projects from pillar to pylon.
I have tired the eyes of the mind
    regarding the .colours and lights.
I have felt for His Wounds
    in nozzles and containers.
I have wondered for the automatic devices.
I have tested the inane patterns
    without prejudice.
I have been on my guard
    not to condemn the unfamiliar.
For it is easy to miss Him
    at the turn of a civilisation.
    I have watched the wheels go round in case I might see
the living creatures like the appearance of lamps, in case I
might see the Living God projected from the Machine. I
have said to the perfected steel, be my sister and for the
glassy towers I thought I felt some beginnings of His
creature, but A, a, a, Domine Deus, my hands found the
glazed work unrefined and the terrible crystal a stage-
paste . . . Eia, Domine Deus.

F. R. SCOTT

b. 1899

Bonne Entente
(or, 'One man's meat is another man's poisson', A. Lismer)

The advantages of living with two cultures
Strike one at every turn,
Especially when one finds a notice in an office building:
'This elevator will not run on Ascension Day';
Or reads in the *Montreal Star:*
'Tomorrow being the Feast of the Immaculate
    Conception,
There will be no collection of garbage in the city';
Or sees on the restaurant menu the bilingual dish:
        DEEP APPLE PIE
    TARTE AUX POMMES PROFONDES

ANONYMOUS

20th century

Once in a saintly passion

Once in a saintly passion
I cried with desperate grief,
'O Lord my heart is black with guile,
Of sinners I am chief.'
Then stopped my guardian angel
And whispered from behind:
'Vanity, my little man;
You're nothing of the kind.'

LANGSTON HUGHES

1902-67

Madam and the Minister

Reverend Butler came by
My house last week.
He said, Have you got
A little time to speak?

He said, I am interested
In your soul.
Has it been saved,
Or is your heart stone-cold?

I said, Reverend,
I'll have you know
I was baptized
Long ago.

He said, What have you
Done since then?
I said, None of your
Business, friend.

He said, Sister
Have you back-slid?
I said, It felt good —
If I did!

He said, Sister,
Come time to die,
The Lord will surely
Ask you why!

I'm gonna pray
For you!
Goodbye!

I felt kinder sorry
I talked that way
After Rev. Butler
Went away —
So I ain't in no mood
For sin today.

STEVIE SMITH

1902-71

The Heavenly City

I sigh for the heavenly country,
Where the heavenly people pass,
And the sea is as quiet as a mirror
Of beautiful, beautiful glass.

I walk in the heavenly field,
With lilies and poppies bright,
I am dressed in a heavenly coat
Of polished white.

When I walk in the heavenly parkland
My feet on the pastures are bare,
Tall waves the grass, but no harmful
Creature is there.

At night I fly over the house tops,
And stand on the bright moony beams;
Gold are all heaven's rivers,
And silver her streams.

The Weak Monk

The monk sat in his den,
He took the mighty pen
And wrote 'Of God and Men.'

One day the thought struck him
It was not according to Catholic doctrine;
His blood ran dim.

He wrote till he was ninety years old,
Then he shut the book with a clasp of gold
And buried it under the sheep fold.

He'd enjoyed it so much, he loved to plod,
And he thought he'd a right to expect that God
Would rescue his book alive from the sod.

Of course it rotted in the snow and rain;
No one will   ever know now what he wrote of God
    and men.
For this the monk is to blame.

RICHARD EBERHART

b. 1904

If I could only live at the pitch that is near madness

If I could only live at the pitch that is near madness
When everything is as it was in my childhood
Violent, vivid, and of infinite possibility:
That the sun and the moon broke over my head.

Then I cast time out of the trees and fields,
Then I stood immaculate in the Ego;
Then I eyed the world with all delight,
Reality was the perfection of my sight.

And time has big handles on the hands,
Fields and trees a way of being themselves.
I saw battalions of the race of mankind
Standing stolid, demanding a moral answer.

I gave the moral answer and I died
And into a realm of complexity came
Where nothing is possible but necessity
And the truth wailing there like a red babe.

PATRICK KAVANAGH

1905-67

Pegasus

My soul was an old horse
Offered for sale in twenty fairs.
I offered him to the Church — the buyers
Were little men who feared his unusual airs.
One said: 'Let him remain unbid
In the wind and rain and hunger
Of sin and we will get him —
With the winkers thrown in — for nothing.'

Then the men of State looked at
What I'd brought for sale.
One minister, wondering if
Another horse-body would fit the tail
That he'd kept for sentiment —
The relic of his own soul —
Said, 'I will graze him in lieu of his labour'.
I lent him for a week or more
And he came back a hurdle of bones,
Starved, overworked, in despair.
I nursed him on the roadside grass
To shape him for another fair.

I lowered my price. I stood him where
The broken-winded, spavined stand
And crooked shopkeepers said that he
Might do a season on the land —
But not for high-paid work in towns.
He'd do a tinker, possibly.
I begged, 'O make some offer now,
A soul is a poor man's tragedy.

He'll draw your dungiest cart,' I said,
'Show you short cuts to Mass,
Teach weather lore, at night collect
Bad debts from poor men's grass'.
               And they would not.

            Where the
Tinkers quarrel I went down
With my horse, my soul.
I cried, 'Who will bid me half a crown?'
From their rowdy bargaining
Not one turned. 'Soul', I prayed,
'I have hawked you through the world
Of Church and State and meanest trade.
But this evening, halter off,
Never again will it go on.
On the south side of ditches
There is grazing of the sun.
No more haggling with the world . . .'

As I said these words he grew
Wings upon his back. Now I may ride him
Every land my imagination knew.

PATRICK KAVANAGH

To be Dead

To be dead is to stop believing in
The masterpieces we will begin tomorrow.
To be an exile is to be a coward,
To know that growth has stopped,
That whatever is done is the end;
Correct the proofs over and over,
Rewrite old poems again and again,
Tell lies to yourself about your achievement:
Ten printed books on the shelves.
Though you know that no-one loves you for what you
    have done
But for what you might do.

And you, perhaps, take up religion bitterly
Which you laughed at in your youth,
Well not actually laughed
But it wasn't your kind of truth.

VERNON WATKINS

b. 1906

The Healing of the Leper

O, have you seen the leper healed,
And fixed your eyes upon his look?
There is the book of God revealed.
And God has made no other book.

The withered hand which time interred
Grasps in a moment the unseen.
The word we had not heard, is heard:
What we are then, we had not been.

Plotinus, preaching on heaven's floor,
Could not give praise like that loud cry
Bursting the bondage of death's door;
For we die once; indeed we die.

What Sandro Botticelli found
Rose from the river where we bathe:
Music the air, the stream, the ground;
Music the dove, the rock, the faith:

And all that music whirled upon
The eyes' deep-sighted, burning rays,
Where all the prayers of labours done
Are resurrected into praise.

But look: his face is like a mask
Surrounded by the beat of wings.
Because he knows that ancient task
His true transfiguration springs.

All fires the prophets' words contained
Fly to those eyes, transfixed above.
Their awful precept has remained:
'Be nothing first; and then, be love.'

LEO KENNEDY

b. 1907

Words for a Resurrection

Each pale Christ stirring underground
Splits the brown casket of its root,
Wherefrom the rousing soil upthrusts
A narrow, pointed shoot,

And bones long quiet under frost
Rejoice as bells precipitate
The loud ecstatic sundering,
The hour inviolate.

This Man of April walks again —
Such marvel does the time allow —
With laughter in His blessed bones,
And lilies on His brow.

W. H. AUDEN

1907-73

We Demand a Miracle

Alone, alone, about a dreadful wood
Of conscious evil runs a lost mankind,
Dreading to find its Father lest it find
The Goodness it has dreaded is not good:
Alone, alone, about our dreadful wood.

Where is that Law for which we broke our own,
Where now that Justice for which Flesh resigned
Her hereditary right to passion, Mind
His will to absolute power? Gone. Gone.
Where is that Law for which we broke our own?

The Pilgrim Way has led to the Abyss.
Was it to meet such grinning evidence
We left our richly odoured ignorance?
Was the triumphant answer to be this?
The Pilgrim Way has led to the Abyss.

We who must die demand a miracle.
How could the Eternal do a temporal act,
The Infinite become a finite fact?
Nothing can save us that is possible:
We who must die demand a miracle.

THEODORE ROETHKE

1908-63

What Can I Tell My Bones?

1

Beginner,
Perpetual beginner,
The soul knows not what to believe,
In its small folds, stirring sluggishly,
In the least place of its life,
A pulse beyond nothingness,
A fearful ignorance.

> Before the moon draws back,
> Dare I blaze like a tree?

In a world always late afternoon,
In the circular smells of a slow wind,
I listen to the weeds' vesperal whine,
Longing for absolutes that never come.
And shapes make me afraid:
The dance of natural objects in the mind,
The immediate sheen, the reality of straw,
The shadows, crawling down a sunny wall.

> A bird sings out in solitariness
> A thin harsh song. The day dies in a child.
> How close we are to the sad animals!
> I need a pool; I need a puddle's calm.

O my bones,
Beware those perpetual beginnings,
Thinning the soul's substance;
The swan's dread of the darkening shore,

Or these insects pulsing near my skin,
The songs from a spiral tree.

> Fury of wind, and no apparent wind,
> A gust blowing the leaves suddenly upward,
> A vine lashing in dry fury,
> A man chasing a cat,
> With a broken umbrella,
> Crying softly.

2

It is difficult to say all things are well,
When the worst is about to arrive;
It is fatal to woo yourself,
However graceful the posture.

> Loved heart, what can I say?
> When I was a lark, I sang;
> When I was a worm, I devoured.

> The self says, I am;
> The heart says, I am less;
> The spirit says, you are nothing.

Mist alters the rocks. What can I tell my bones?
My desire's a wind trapped in a cave.
The spirit declares itself to these rocks.
I'm a small stone, loose in the shale.
Love is my wound.

The wide streams go their way,
The pond lapses back into a glassy silence.
The cause of God in me — has it gone?
Do these bones live? Can I live with these bones?

Mother, mother of us all, tell me where I am!
O to be delivered from the rational into the realm of pure
    song,
My face on fire, close to the points of a star,
A learned nimble girl,
Not drearily bewitched,
But sweetly daft.

    To try to become like God
    Is far from becoming God.
    O, but I seek and care!

    I rock in my own dark,
    Thinking, God has need of me.
    The dead love the unborn.

3

Weeds turn toward the wind weed-skeletons.
How slowly all things alter.
Existence dares perpetuate a soul,
A wedge of heaven's light, autumnal song.
I hear a beat of birds, the plangent wings
That disappear into a waning moon;
The barest speech of light among the stones.

    To what more vast permission have I come?
    When I walk past a vat, water joggles,
    I no longer cry for green in the midst of cinders,
    Or dream of the dead, and their holes.
    Mercy has many arms.

Instead of a devil with horns, I prefer a serpent with
    scales;
In temptation, I rarely seek counsel;
A prisoner of smells, I would rather eat than pray.
I'm released from the dreary dance of opposites.

The wind rocks with my wish; the rain shields me;
I live in light's extreme; I stretch in all directions;
Sometimes I think I'm several.

    The sun! The sun! And all we can become!
    And the time ripe for running to the moon!
    In the long fields, I leave my father's eye;
    And shake the secrets from my deepest bones;
    My spirit rises with the rising wind;

    I'm thick with leaves and tender as a dove,
    I take the liberties a short life permits —
    I seek my own meekness;
    I recover my tenderness by long looking.
    By midnight I love everything alive.
    Who took the darkness from the air?
    I'm wet with another life.
    Yea. I have gone and stayed.

    What came to me vaguely is now clear,
    As if released by a spirit,
    Or agency outside me.
    Unprayed-for,
    And final.

A. M. KLEIN

1909-72

The Still Small Voice

The candles splutter; and the kettle hums;
The heirloomed clock enumerates the tribes,
Upon the wine-stained table-cloth lie crumbs
Of matzoh whose wide scattering describes
Jews driven in far lands upon this earth.
The kettle hums; the candles splutter; and
Winds whispering from shutters tell re-birth
Of beauty rising in an eastern land,
Of paschal sheep driven in cloudy droves;
Of almond-blossoms colouring the breeze;
Of vineyards upon verdant terraces;
Of golden globes in orient orange-groves.
And those assembled at the table dream
Of small schemes that an April wind doth scheme,
And cry from out the sleep assailing them:
Jerusalem! Jerusalem! Jerusalem!

W. HART-SMITH

b. 1911

Eathelswith

Rode her horse sidesaddle
as is seemly in a gentlewoman,
more so as a Queen
making pilgrimage to Rome.

Frail, gentle, beautiful,
fair of hair, blue of eye,
fragile, small,
rocking on the huge rump

of a big bay horse:
Ethel, Eathelswith
Regina. The bezel is the part of a ring

that holds the stone. A
plough turned in a field a gold ring
inscribed with the Agnus Dei,
and the letters A and D, the latter

with a lateral stroke
to indicate THORN,
a sound the Romans did not have;
and on the inside,

'Eathelswith Regina' (Eathelswith,
sister of King Alfred,
wife of Burhred,
King of Mercia?)

She, on her way to Rome,
having a presentiment of death,
offered her gold ring
at a wayside shrine in Yorkshire.

Died on the journey. Buried at Pavia.
Ring turned by the plough keel
between Aberford and Sherburn.
Farmboy saw it,

a glint of gold in the furrow,
and picked it up.
A priest, it would seem,
to record the gift, the offering,

engraved her name
crudely on the inside

— EA
DELSVID
REGNA

Eathelswith Regina (Ethel,
Lamb of God),
to Rome for her shriving,
her soul's sake,

retainers few,
brave and God-trusting.
Died
on the journey.

F. T. PRINCE

b. 1912

The Question

And so we too came where the rest have come,
To where each dreamed, each drew, the other home
From all distractions to the other's breast,
Where each had found, each was, the wild bird's nest.
For that we came, and knew that we must know
The thing we knew of but we did not know.

We said then, What if this were now no more
Than a faint shade of what we dreamed before?
If love should here find little joy or none,
And done, it were as if it were not done,
Would we not love still? What if none can know
The thing we know of but we do not know?

For we know nothing but that, long ago,
We learnt to love God whom we cannot know.
I touch your eyelids that one day must close,
Your lips as perishable as a rose:
And say that all must fade, before we know
The thing we know of but we do not know.

ANNE RIDLER

b. 1912

Christmas and Common Birth

Christmas declares the glory of the flesh:
And therefore a European might wish
To celebrate it not in midwinter but in spring,
When physical life is strong,
When the consent to live is forced even on the young,
Juice is in the soil, the leaf, the vein,
Sugar flows to movement in limbs and brain.
Also, before a birth, in nourishing the child,
We turn again to the earth
With unusual longing — to what is rich, wild,
Substantial: scents that have been stored and
        strengthened
In apple lofts, the underwash of woods, and in barns;
Drawn through the lengthened root; pungent in cones
(While the fir wood stands waiting; the beech wood
        aspiring,
Each in a different silence), and breaking out in spring
With scent sight sound indivisible in song.

Yet if you think again
It is good that Christmas comes at the dark dream of
        the year
That might wish to sleep for ever.

For birth is awaking, birth is effort and pain;
And now at midwinter are the hints, inklings
(Sodden primrose, honeysuckle greening)
That sleep must be broken.
To bear new life or learn to live is an exacting joy:
The whole self must waken; you cannot predict the way

It will happen, or master the responses beforehand.
For any birth makes an inconvenient demand;
Like all holy things
It is frequently a nuisance, and its needs never end;
Strange freedom it brings: we should welcome release
From its long merciless rehearsal of peace.

So Christ comes
At the iron senseless time, comes
To force the glory into frozen veins:
His warmth wakes
Green life glazed in the pool, wakes
All calm and crystal trance with living pains.

And each year
In seasonal growth is good — year
That lacking love is a stale story at best;
By God's birth
All common birth is holy; birth
Is all at Christmas time and wholly blest.

R. S. THOMAS

b. 1913

In a Country Church

To one kneeling down no word came,
Only the wind's song, saddening the lips
Of the grave saints, rigid in glass;
Or the dry whisper of unseen wings,
Bats not angels, in the high roof.

Was he balked by silence? He kneeled long,
And saw love in a dark crown
Of thorns blazing, and a winter tree
Golden with fruit of a man's body.

R. S. THOMAS

Kneeling

Moments of great calm
Kneeling before an altar
Of wood in a stone church
In summer, waiting for the God
To speak; the air a staircase
For silence; the sun's light
Ringing me, as though I acted
A great role. And the audiences
Still; all that close throng
Of spirits waiting, as I,
For the message.

              Prompt me, God;
But not yet. When I speak,
Though it be you who speak
Through me, something is lost.
The meaning is in the waiting.

JOHN BERRYMAN

1914-72

From *The Dream Songs*, 153

I'm cross with god who has wrecked this generation.
First he seized Ted, then Richard, Randall, and now
   Delmore.
In between he gorged on Sylvia Plath.
That was a first rate haul. He left alive
fools I could number like a kitchen knife
but Lowell he did not touch.

Somewhere the enterprise continues, not —
yellow the sun lies on the baby's blouse —
in Henry's staggered thought.
I suppose the word would be, we must submit.
Later.
I hang, and I will not be part of it.

A friend of Henry's contrasted God's career
with Mozart's, leaving Henry with nothing to say
but praise for a word so apt.
We suffer on, a day, a day, a day.
And never again can come, like a man slapped,
news like this

JOHN BERRYMAN

From *The Dream Songs*, 156

I give in. I must not leave the scene of this same death
as most of me strains to.
There are all the problems to be sorted out,
the fate of the soul, what it was all about
during its being, and whether he was drunk
at 4 a.m. on the wrong floor too

fighting for air, tearing his sorry clothes
with his visions dying O and O I mourn
again this complex death
Almost my oldest friend should never have been born
to this terrible end, out of which what grows
but an unshaven, dissheveled *corpse?*

The spirit & the joy, in memory
live of him on, the young will read his young verse
for as long as such things go:
why then do I despair, miserable Henry
who *knew* him all so long, for better & worse
and nearly would follow him below.

RANDALL JARRELL

1914-65

The Orient Express

One looks from the train
Almost as one looked as a child. In the sunlight
What I see still seems to me plain,
I am safe; but at evening
As the lands darken, a questioning
Precariousness comes over everything.

Once after a day of rain
I lay longing to be cold; and after a while
I was cold again, and hunched shivering
Under the quilt's many colors, gray
With the dull ending of the winter day.
Outside me there were a few shapes
Of chairs and tables, things from a primer;
Outside the window
There were the chairs and tables of the world . . . .
I saw that the world
That had seemed to me the plain
Gray mask of all that was strange
Behind it — all of that *was* — was all.

But it is beyond belief.
One thinks, "Behind everything
An unforced joy, an unwilling
Sadness (a willing sadness, a forced joy)
Moves changelessly"; one looks from the train
And there is something, the same thing
Behind everything: all these little villages,
A passing woman, a field of grain,
The man who says good-bye to his wife —

A path through a wood full of lives, and the train
Passing, after all unchangeable
And not now ever to stop, like a heart —

It is like any other work of art.
It is and never can be changed.
Behind everything there is always
The unknown unwanted life.

DYLAN THOMAS

1914-53

And Death Shall Have No Dominion

And death shall have no dominion.
Dead men naked they shall be one
With the man in the wind and the west moon;
When their bones are picked clean and the clean bones
    gone,
They shall have stars at elbow and foot;
Though they go mad they shall be sane,
Though they sink through the sea they shall rise again;
Though lovers be lost love shall not;
And death shall have no dominion.

And death shall have no dominion.
Under the windings of the sea
They lying long shall not die windily;
Twisting on racks when sinews give way,
Strapped to a wheel, yet they shall not break;
Faith in their hands shall snap in two,
And the unicorn evils run them through;
Split all ends up they shan't crack;
And death shall have no dominion.

And death shall have no dominion.
No more may gulls cry at their ears
Or waves break loud on the seashores;
Where blew a flower may a flower no more
Lift its head to the blows of the rain;
Though they be mad and dead as nails,
Heads of the characters hammer through daisies;
Break in the sun till the sun breaks down,
And death shall have no dominion.

JUDITH WRIGHT

b. 1915

Eli, Eli

To see them go by drowning in the river—
soldiers and elders drowning in the river,
the pitiful women drowning in the river,
the children's faces staring from the river—
that was his cross, and not the cross they gave him.

To hold the invisible wand, and not save them —
to know them turned to death, and yet not save them;
only to cry to them and not to save them,
knowing that no one but themselves could save them —
this was the wound, more than the wound they dealt him.

To hold out love and know they would not take it,
to hold out faith and know they dared not take it—
the invisible wand, and none would see or take it,
all he could give, and there was none to take it—
thus they betrayed him, not with the tongue's betrayal.

He watched, and they were drowning in the river;
faces like sodden flowers in the river—
faces of children moving in the river;
and all the while, he knew there was no river.

ROBERT LOWELL

b. 1917

Our Lady of Walsingham

There once the penitents took off their shoes
And then walked barefoot the remaining mile;
And the small trees, a stream and hedgerows file
Slowly along the munching English lane,
Like cows to the old shrine, until you lose
Track of your dragging pain.
The stream flows down under the druid tree,
Shiloah's whirlpools gurgle and make glad
The castle of God. Sailor, you were glad
And whistled Sion by that stream. But see:

Our Lady, too small for her canopy,
Sits near the altar. There's no comeliness
At all or charm in that expressionless
Face with its heavy eyelids. As before,
This face, for centuries a memory,
Non est species, neque decor,
Expressionless, expresses God: it goes
Past castled Sion. She knows what God knows,
Not Calvary's Cross nor crib at Bethlehem
Now, and the world shall come to Walsingham.

JAMES McAULEY

1917-1976

Late Sunday Afternoon

Muddy pools along the road
Mirror with a failing light
Grey ragged clouds and a pure height
Which at a passing wheel explode.

In the wet park July feels strange.
Bronze foil and russet overlap
New shoots of green. Black starlings clap
Their yellow beaks, announcing change.

Candles gleam, a bell is rung,
The faithful move towards the bread.
I shudder with desire and dread,
Tasting death upon my tongue.

Jesus

Touching Ezekiel his workman's hand
Kindled the thick and thorny characters;
And seraphim that seemed a thousand eyes,
Flying leopards, wheels and basilisks,
Creatures of power and of judgment, soared
From his finger-point, emblazoning the skies.

Then turning from the book he rose and walked
Among the stones and beasts and flowers of earth;
They turned their muted faces to their Lord,
Their real faces, seen by God alone;
And people moved before him undisguised;
He thrust his speech among them like a sword.

And when a dove came to his hand he knew
That hell was opening behind its wings.
He thanked the messenger and let it go;
Spoke to the dust, the fishes and the twelve
As if they understood him equally,
And told them nothing that they wished to know.

ROBERT DUNCAN

b. 1919

The Ballad of Mrs Noah

Mrs Noah in the Ark
wove a great nightgown out of the dark,
did Mrs Noah,

had her own hearth in the Holy Boat,
two cats, two books, two cooking pots,
had Mrs Noah,

two pints of porter, two pecks of peas,
and a stir in her stew of memories.

Oh, that was a town, said Mrs Noah,
that the Lord in His wrath
did up and drown!

I liked its windows and I liked its trees.
Save me a little, Lord, I prayd on my knees.
And now, Lord save me, I've two of each!
apple, apricot, cherry and peach.

How shall I manage it? I've two of them all —
hairy, scaly, leathery, slick,
fluttery, buttery, thin and thick,
shaped like a stick, shaped like a ball,
too tiny to see, and much too tall.

I've all that I askd for and more and more,
windows and chimneys, and a great store
of needles and pins, of outs and ins,
and a regular forgive-us for some of my sins.

She wove a great nightgown out of the dark
decorated like a Sunday Park
with clouds of black thread to remember her grief
sewn about with bright flowers to give relief,

and, in a grim humor, a border all round
with the little white bones of the wicked drownd.

Tell me, Brother, what do you see?
said Mrs Noah to the Lowly Worm.

O Mother, the Earth is black, black.
To my crawlly bride and lowly me
the Earth is bitter as can be
where the Dead lie down and never come back,
said the blind Worm.

Tell me, Brother, what do *you* see?
said Mrs Noah to the sleeping Cat.

O Mother, the weather is dreadful wet.
I'll keep house for you wherever you'll be.
I'll sit by the fireside and be your pet.
And as long as I'm dry I'll purr for free,
said snug-loving Cat.

Tell me, Brother, has the flood gone?
said Mrs Noah to the searching crow.

No. No. No home in sight.
I fly thru the frightful waste alone,
said the carrion Crow.
The World is an everlasting Night.

Now that can't be true, Noah, Old Noah,
said the good Housewife to her good Spouse.
How long must we go in this floating House?
growing old and hope cold,
Husband, without new land?

And then Glory-Be with a rainbow to-boot!
the Dove returned with an Olive Shoot.

Tell me, Brother, what have we here,
my Love? to the Dove said Mrs Noah.

It's a Branch of All-Cheer
you may wear on your nightgown all the long year
as a boa, Mrs Noah, said, the Dove,
with God's Love!

> Then out from the Ark
> in her nightgown all dark
> with only her smile to betoken the Day
> and a wreath-round of olive leaves.

Mrs. Noah stepped down
into the same old wicked repenting
Lord-Will-We-Ever recently recovered
comfortable World-Town.

O where have you been, Mother Noah, Mother Noah?
I've had a great Promise for only Tomorrow.
In the Ark of Sleep I've been on a sail
over the wastes of the world's sorrow.

And the Promise? the Tomorrow? Mother Noah, Mother
    Noah?
Ah! the Rainbow's awake
and we will not fail!

GWEN HARWOOD

b. 1920

Triste, Triste

In the space between love and sleep
when heart mourns in its prison
eyes against shoulder keep
their blood-black curtains tight.
Body rolls back like a stone, and risen
spirit walks to Easter light;

away from its tomb of bone,
away from the guardian tents
of eyesight, walking alone
to unbearable light with angelic
gestures. The fallen instruments
of its passion lie in the relic

darkness of sleep and love.
And heart from its prison cries
to the spirit walking above:
'I was with you in agony.
Remember your promise of paradise,'
and hammers and hammers, 'Remember me.'

DANIEL BERRIGAN

b. 1921

The Face of Christ

The tragic beauty of the face of Christ
shines in the face of man;

the abandoned old live on
in shabby rooms, far from inner comfort.
Outside, in the street
din and purpose, the world like a fiery animal
reined in by youth. Within
a pallid tiring heart
shuffles about its dwelling.

Nothing, or so little, come of life's promise.
Out of broken men, despised minds
what does one make —
a roadside show, a graveyard of the heart?

The Christian God reproves
faithless ranting minds
crushing like upper and lower stones
all life between;
Christ, fowler of street and hedgerow
of cripples and the distempered old
— eyes blind as woodknots,
tongues tight as immigrants —
takes in His gospel net
all the hue and cry of existence.

Heaven, of such imperfection,
wary, ravaged, wild?

Yes. Compel them in.

PHILIP LARKIN

b. 1922

An Arundel Tomb

Side by side, their faces blurred,
The earl and countess lie in stone,
Their proper habits vaguely shown
As jointed armour, stiffened pleat,
And that faint hint of the absurd —
The little dogs under their feet.

Such plainness of the pre-baroque
Hardly involves the eye, until
It meets his left-hand gauntlet, still
Clasped empty in the other; and
One sees, with a sharp tender shock,
His hand withdrawn, holding her hand.

They would not think to lie so long.
Such faithfulness in effigy
Was just a detail friends would see:
A sculptor's sweet commissioned grace
Thrown off in helping to prolong
The Latin names around the base.

They would not guess how early in
Their supine stationary voyage
The air would change to soundless damage,
Turn the old tenantry away;
How soon succeeding eyes begin
To look, not read. Rigidly they

Persisted, linked, through lengths and breadths
Of time. Snow fell, undated. Light

Each summer thronged the glass. A bright
Litter of birdcalls strewed the same
Bone-riddled ground. And up the paths
The endless altered people came,

Washing at their identity.
Now, helpless in the hollow of
An unarmorial age, a trough
Of smoke in slow suspended skeins
Above their scrap of history,
Only an attitude remains:

Time has transfigured them into
Untruth. The stone fidelity
They hardly meant has come to be
Their final blazon, and to prove
Our almost-instinct almost true:
What will survive of us is love.

Days

What are days for?
Days are where we live.
They come, they wake us
Time and time over.
They are to be happy in:
Where can we live but days?

Ah, solving that question
Brings the priest and the doctor
In their long coats
Running over the fields.

JOHN ORMOND

b. 1923

To a Nun
After the 15th Century Welsh

Please God, forsake your water and dry bread
And fling the bitter cress you eat aside.
Put by your rosary. In Mary's name
Leave chanting creeds to all those monks in Rome.
Spring is at work in woodlands bright with sun;
Springtime's not made for living like a nun.
Your faith, my fairest lady, your religion
Show but a single face of love's medallion.
Slip on this ring and this green gown, these laces:
The wood is furnitured with resting places.
Hide in the birch tree's shade — upon your knees
Murmur the mass of cuckoos, litanies
Of spring's green foliage. There's no sacrilege
If we find heaven here against the hedge.
Remember Ovid's book and Ovid's truth:
There's such a thing as having too much faith.
Let us discover the shapes, the earthly signs
Of our true selves, our souls, among the vines.
For surely God and all his saints above,
High in their other heaven, pardon love.

JOHN HAINES

b. 1924

The Wreck

The Church, like a wreck blown ashore
from the Middle Ages,
battering on a shoal at Finisterre . . .

The seams have opened,
and the sea, like a luminous window
falling away, flashes briefly
with ikons, chalices, gold candlesticks.

Angels and saints, their faces
crusted with salt,
draw near to the flooded railing.
They try to sing — the wind,
full of a wintry fervour,
whips the kyries from broken spars.

And the figurehead on a cross
has never moved . . .

A couch mourns in the littered shallows;
unwieldy shapes, driftwood and sea-coal,
groan and struggle to their feet,
survivors from a shipwreck of souls.

VINCENT BUCKLEY

b. 1925

Places
For J. Golden, S.J.

I

Walking at ease where the great houses
Shelter the assorted trees that someone
Planted, once, to shelter them, I do
My voluntary patrol. The wind moves
Houses and trees together, till they breathe
As though I breathed with them, systole, diastole
Of the built and the growing.
Fair enough. We used to picture
Paradise both as a garden and a city.
Here it's a green hardihood, a tender
Rallying beyond concupiscence.
So I patrol. There's not a soul in sight.
It was an older, foreign voice that cried
'The swarm of bees enfolds the ancient hive'.

II

But love is a harsh and pure honey.
The world is brought alive with us
So many times. One night I learned the resurrection
In still water. Sea-mist moves
On a land that in its steeped
Peach-dark fruits,
Resin,
Pods,
Is warm as blood.
I lean on the bridge, looking down.
Under the utter moon all things reach

Their height in water; there the thin
Unbreathing tree touches the depth of cloud
Downward; there light vibrates in the sky.
In this voluptuous arrest of colour
I still feel the day's heat on my eyelids.
At noon the summer webbed us in; but now
I almost smell the next year's seed.

III

Bound from Mass, my blood fresh as the sea.
In the city light there are pools, deep-groined,
Where the gilled bodies leap down and glide;
And the sea-smell, drifting like the sounds of sleep,
Gives air a distance, not a shape,
And light itself is recreated, made
Native to all bodies. I think how once,
Hardly thinking, in a strange church,
A man, forgetting the common rubric, prayed
'O God, make me worthy of the world',
And felt his own silence sting his tongue.

JEROME KIELY

b. 1925

For a Young Cistercian Monk

He bowed to me when he brought the wine at Mass,
a young monk with an age of graciousness,
   his white robes gesturing eight hundred years of awe,
bowed low, a beetle clawed in humbleness,
   and I must stand erect by splint of canon law.

He bowed again before he washed my hands,
his robes like white waves curling for a flat of sands.
   Worshipful shepherd in a curving crèche
he saw my mask, not me. The Rule's commands
   hunched him like dolmen to defer to mortal flesh.

I bow to him with all the self I've bent
into these lines; I curtsy to his robe, the tent
   in which he stores his trackless life; I bow
to his long sleeves, wings of the cormorant
   that bates with God upon the ebbing tide of now.

I bow to princedom in his circled hair;
I yield to genius in his geometry of prayer,
   his angled cowl and arc of song at Terce;
I am but knee, he is the holy stair;
   I bow to him with this obeisance of verse.

FRANCIS WEBB

1925-73

Five Days Old
(for Christopher John)

Christmas is in the air.
You are given into my hands
Out of quietest, loneliest lands.
My trembling is all my prayer.
To blown straw was given
All the fullness of Heaven.

The tiny, not the immense,
Will teach our groping eyes.
So the absorbed skies
Bleed stars of innocence.
So cloud-voice in war and trouble
Is at last Christ in the stable.

Now wonderingly engrossed
In your fearless delicacies,
I am launched upon sacred seas,
Humbly and utterly lost
In the mystery of creation,
Bells, bells of ocean.

Too pure for my tongue to praise,
That sober, exquisite yawn
Or the gradual, generous dawn
At an eyelid, maker of days:
To shrive my thought for perfection
I must breathe old tempests of action

For the snowflakes and face of love,
Windfall and word of truth,
Honour close to death.
O eternal truthfulness, Dove,
Tell me what I hold —
Myrrh? Frankincense? Gold?

If this is man, then the danger
And fear are as lights of the inn,
Faint and remote as sin
Out here by the manger.
In the sleeping, weeping weather
We shall all kneel down together.

JAMES BAXTER

1926-73

From *Autumn Testament*

After writing for an hour in the presbytery
I visit the church, that dark loft of God,

And make my way uphill. The grass is soaking my
    trousers,
The night dark, the rain falling out of the night,

And the old fears walk side by side with me,
Either the heavy thump of an apple

Hitting the ground, or the creaking of the trees,
Or the presence of two graveyards,

The new one at the house, the old one on the hill
That I have never entered. Heaven is light

And Hell is darkness, so the Christmen say,
But this dark is the belly of the whale

In which I, Jonah, have to make my journey
Till the fear has gone. Fear is the only enemy.

ROBERT CREELEY

b. 1926

Fancy

Do you know what
the truth is,
what's rightly
or wrongly said,

what is wiseness,
or rightness, what
wrong, or well-
done if it is,

or is not, done.
I thought.
I thought and
thought and thought.

In a place
I was sitting,
and there
it was, a little

faint thing
hardly felt, a
kind of small
nothing.

GUNTER GRASS

b. 1927

Hymn

As complicated as a nightingale,
as tinny as,
kind-hearted as,
as crease-proof, as traditional,
as green grave sour, as streaky,
as symmetrical,
as hairy,
as near the water, true to the wind,
as fireproof, frequently turned over,
as childishly easy, well-thumbed as,
as new and creaking, expensive as,
as deeply cellared, domestic as,
as easily lost, shiny with use,
as thinly blown, as snow-chilled as,
as independent, as mature,
as heartless as,
as mortal as,
as simple as my soul.

ANNE SEXTON

b. 1928

For God While Sleeping

Sleeping in fever, I am unfit
to know just who you are:
hung up like a pig on exhibit,
the delicate wrists,
the beard drooling blood and vinegar;
hooked to your own weight,
jolting toward death under your nameplate.

Everyone in this crowd needs a bath.
I am dressed in rags.
The mother wears blue. You grind your teeth
and with each new breath
your jaws gape and your diaper sags.
I am not to blame
for all this. I do not know your name.

Skinny man, you are somebody's fault.
You ride on dark poles —
a wooden bird that a trader built
for some fool who felt
that he could make the flight. Now you roll
in your sleep, seasick
on your own breathing, poor old convict.

THOM GUNN

b. 1929

Jesus and His Mother

My only son, more God's than mine,
Stay in this garden ripe with pears.
The yielding of their substance wears
A modest and contented shine:
And when they weep with age, not brine
But lazy syrup are their tears.
'I am my own and not my own.'

He seemed much like another man,
That silent foreigner who trod
Ouside my door with lily rod:
How could I know what I began
Meeting the eyes more furious than
The eyes of Joseph, those of God?
I was my own and not my own.

And who are these twelve labouring men?
I do not understand your words:
I taught you speech, we named the birds,
You marked their big migrations then
Like any child. So turn again
To silence from the place of crowds.
'I am my own and not my own.'

Why are you sullen when I speak?
Here are your tools, the saw and knife
And hammer on your bench. Your life
Is measured here in week and week
Planed as the furniture you make,
And I will teach you like a wife
To be my own and all my own.

Who like an arrogant wind blown
Where he may please, needs no content?
Yet I remember how you went
To speak with scholars in furred gown.
I hear an outcry in the town;
Who carries that dark instrument?
'One all his own and not his own.'

Treading the green and nimble sward
I stare at a strange shadow thrown.
Are you the boy I bore alone
No doctor near to cut the cord?
I cannot reach to call you Lord,
Answer me as my only son.
'I am my own and not my own.'

PETER PORTER

b. 1929

At Whitechurch Canonicorum

This is a land permutating green
and can afford its pagan ghostly state.
Only from the recurring dead between
the well-dark hedge and talking gate
can mystery come, the church's graveyard,
where now the sun tops the stones and makes
shadows long as a man work as hard
to live as he did, rotting there till he wakes.

That he will wake to trumpets they believed
or tried to who bought him ground to hold.
His dead eye takes in the high coiffure of leaves,
the pebble-dash tower, the numbers in gold
upon the clock face. For once he has reason —
this undistinguished church, whose frown
lies in the lap of Dorset rebuking each season
its appropriate worldliness, has a saint, pale and home-
    grown.

Saint Candida, white in her Latin and cement tomb,
has lived here since rumour was born.
A woman's pelvis needs only the little room
of a casket to heal the flesh it was torn
from: an enlightened bishop lifted up her lid
and pronounced her genuine, a lady's
bones who if she healed as they say she did
I ask to help me escape the further elbowing of Hades.

I tried to put once, while no one was about,
in the holes for the petitioners' limbs,
the front of my trousers, for love locked out
not impotence, and spoke to that air which held hymns
like amber from the stained glass sides
a prayer to the saint to be given love
by the person I loved. That prayer still resides
there unanswered. I gave the iron-studded door a shove

and stood again among the unsaintly dead.
St. Candida is also St. Wite,
the Latin derived from the Saxon misread,
the death clothes she sings in as bitter
to her as when her saintly heart stopped.
England has only two saints' relics confirmed
and hers are one. Three times now I've dropped
by at Whitechurch and asked her her easiest terms

for assistance. The old iron trees tend to roar
in the wind and the cloud seems unusually low
on the fields, even in summer. The weight of before
stands here for faith; so many are born and go
back, marvellous like painting or stones:
I offer my un-numinous body to the saint's care
and pray on my feet to her merciful bones
for ease of the ulcer of feeling, the starch of despair.

BRUCE DAWE
b. 1930

And a Good Friday Was Had by All

You men there, keep those women back
and God Almighty he laid down
on the crossed timber and old Silenus
my offsider look at me as if to say
nice work for soldiers, your mind's not your own
once you sign that dotted line Ave Caesar
and all that malarkey Imperator Rex

well this Nazarene
didn't make it any easier
really — not like the ones
who kick up a fuss so you can
do your block and take it out on them
                                            Silenus
held the spikes steady and I let fly
with the sledge-hammer, not looking
on the downswing trying hard not to hear
over the women's wailing the bones give way
the iron shocking the dumb wood.

Orders is orders, I said after it was over
nothing personal you understand — we had a
drill-sergeant once thought he was God but he wasn't
a patch on you

then we hauled on the ropes
and he rose in the hot air
like a diver just leaving the springboard, arms spread
so it seemed
over the whole damned creation
over the big men who must have had it in for him
and the curious ones who'll watch anything if it's free
with only the usual women caring anywhere
and a blind man in tears.

BRIAN HIGGINS

1930-65

Genesis

Language is the first perversion of the senses.
The alphabet was written on the gates of Eden.
Reason is an angel in mathematics, a castration in
    literature, and a devil in life.
The first and last speech was a curse.
When the moon was numbered the stars grew pale.
It was God who conspired with Satan in that garden
When, lowering the snake, he sent words to prove the
    Fall.

TED HUGHES

b. 1930

Crow's Theology

Crow realized God loved him —
Otherwise, he would have dropped dead.
So that was proved.
Crow reclined, marvelling, on his heart-beat.

And he realized that God spoke Crow —
Just existing was His revelation.

But what
Loved the stones and spoke stone?
They seemed to exist too.
And what spoke that strange silence
After his clamour of caws faded?

And what loved the shot-pellets
That dribbled from those strung-up mummifying crows?
What spoke the silence of lead?

Crow realized there were two Gods —

One of them much bigger than the other
Loving his enemies
And having all the weapons.

Crow Blacker Than Ever

When God, disgusted with man,
Turned towards heaven.
And man, disgusted with God,
Turned towards Eve,
Things looked like falling apart.

But Crow   Crow
Crow nailed them together,
Nailing Heaven and earth together —

So man cried, but with God's voice.
And God bled, but with man's blood.

Then heaven and earth creaked at the joint
Which became gangrenous and stank —
A horror beyond redemption.

The agony did not diminish.

Man could not be man nor God God.

The agony

Grew.

Crow

Grinned

Crying: 'This is my Creation,'

Flying the black flag of himself.

GEOFFREY HILL

b. 1932

From *Lachrimae* or *Seven Tears Figured in Seven Passionate Pavans*

1. Lachrimae Verae

Crucified Lord, you swim upon your cross
and never move. Sometimes in dreams of hell
the body moves but moves to no avail
and is at one with that eternal loss.

You are the castaway of drowned remorse,
you are the world's atonement on the hill.
This is your body twisted by our skill
into a patience proper for redress.

I cannot turn aside from what I do;
you cannot turn away from what I am.
You do not dwell in me nor I in you

however much I pander to your name
or answer to your lords of revenue,
surrendering the joys that they condemn.

2. Lachrimae Amantis

What is there in my heart that you should sue
so fiercely for its love? What kind of care
brings you as though a stranger to my door
through the long night and in icy dew

seeking the heart that will not harbour you,
that keeps itself religiously secure?
At this dark solstice filled with frost and fire
your passion's ancient wounds must bleed
    anew.

So many nights the angel of my house
has fed such urgent comfort through a dream,
whispered 'your lord is coming, he is close'

that I have drowsed half-faithful for a time
bathed in pure tones of promise and remorse:
'tomorrow I shall wake to welcome him.'

FAY ZWICKY

Kaddish

For my Father
born 1903, died at sea, 1967

Lord of the divided, heal!

Father, old ocean's skull making storm calm and the
    waves to sleep,
Visits his first-born, humming in dreams, hiding the
    pearls that were
Behind *Argus,* defunct Melbourne rag. The wireless
    shouts declarations of

War. 'Father,' says the first-born first time around (and
    nine years dead),
Weeping incurable for all his hidden skills. His country's
    Medical Journal
Laid him out amid Sigmoid Volvulus, Light on Gastric
    Problems, Health Services

For Young Children Yesterday Today and Tomorrow
    which is now and now and now and
Never spoke his name which is Father a war having
    happened between her birth, his
Death: Yisborach, v'yistabach, v'yispoar, v'yisroman,
    v'yisnaseh - Hitler is

Dead. The Japanese are different. Let us talk of now.
    The war is ended.
Strangers found you first. Bearing love back, your first-
    born bears their praise

FAY ZWICKY

Into the sun-filled room, hospitals you tended, city
roofs and yards, ethereal rumours.

Gray's Inn Road, Golden Square, St. George's,
Birmingham, Vienna's General, the
Ancient Alfred in Commercial Road where, tearing paper
in controlled strips, your
First-born waited restless and autistic, shredding life,
lives, ours. 'Have to

See a patient. Wait for me,' healing knife ready as the
first-born, girt to kill,
Waited, echoes of letters from Darwin, Borneo, Moratai,
Brunei ('We thought him
Dead but the little Jap sat up with gun in hand and took
a shot at us',) the heat

A pressing fist, swamps, insect life ('A wonderful war'
said his wife who also
Waited) but wait for me wait understand O wait between
the lines unread.
Your first-born did not. Tested instead the knife's weight.

————————

Let in the strangers first: 'Apart from his high degree of
medical skill he
Possessed warmth' (enough to make broken grass live?
rock burst into flower?
Then why was your first-born cold?) But listen again: 'It
was impossible for

Him to be rude, rough, abrupt.' Shy virgin bearing gifts
to the proud first and
Only born wife, black virgin mother. Night must have
come terrible to such a

169

Kingdom. All lampless creatures sighing in their beds,
    stones wailing as the

Mated flew apart in sorrow. Near, apart, fluttered, fell
    apart as feathered
Hopes trembled to earth shaken from the boughs of
    heaven. By day the heart
Was silent, shook in its box of bone, alone fathered
    three black dancing imps,

The wicked, the wise and the simple to jump in the
    house that Jack built: This
Is the priest all shaven and shorn who married the man
    all tattered and torn
Who kissed the maiden all forlorn who slaughtered the
    ox who drank the water

Who put out the fire who burnt the staff who smote the
    dog who bit the cat who
Ate the kid my father bought from the angel of death:
    'Never heard to complain,
Response to inquiry about his health invariably brought
    a retort causing laughter.'

Laughter in the shadow of the fountain, laughter in the
    dying fire, laughter
Shaking in the box of bone, laughter fastened in the
    silent night, laughter
While the children danced from room to room in the
    empty air.

What ailed the sea that it fled? What ailed the mountains,
    the romping lambs
Bought with blood? Tremble, earth, before the Lord of
    the Crow and the Dove
Who turned flint into fountain, created the fruit of the
    vine devoured by the

Fox who bit the dog that worried the cat that killed the
    rat that ate up Jack
Who built the house: Yisgaddal v'yiskaddash sh'meh rabbo
    — miracle of seed,
Mystery of rain, the ripening sun and the failing flesh,
    courses of stars,

Stress from Sinai:

Let (roared God)

    Great big Babylon
    Be eaten up by Persia
    Be eaten up by Greece
    Be eaten up by Rome
    Be eaten up by Ottoman
    Be eaten up by Edom
    Be eaten by Australia
    Where Jack's house shook.

Be (said Jack's Dad)

    Submissive to an elder
    Courteous to the young
    Receive all men with
    Cheerfulness and
    Hold your tongue.

Strangers, remember Jack who did as he was told.

———

To the goddess the blood of all creatures is due for she
    gave it,
Temple and slaughterhouse, maker of curses like worm-
    eaten peas:

As the thunder vanishes, so shall the woman drive them
    away
As wax melts before flame, so let the ungodly perish
    before her:

She is mother of thunder, mother of trees, mother of
    lakes,
Secret springs, gate to the underworld, vessel of
    darkness,

Bearer, transformer, dark nourisher, shelterer, container
    of
Living and dead, coffin of Osiris, dark-egg devourer,
    engenderer,

Nurturer, nurse of the world, many-armed goddess
    girdled by cobras,
Flame-spewer, tiger-tongued queen of the dead and the
    violent dancers.

Mother of songs, dancer of granite, giver of stone —
Let his wife speak:

'Honour thy father and thy mother'
So have I done and done and done — no marriage shall
    ever

Consume the black maidenhead — my parents are heaven
Bound. I shall rejoin them;

Bodies of men shall rejoin severed souls
At the ultimate blast of invisible grace.

Below, I burn,
Naomi of the long brown hair, skull in a Juliet cap.

Do the dead rot? Then rot as I rot as they rot.
'Honour thy Father' sing Armistice bells, *espressivo*.

The stumbling fingers are groping
To pitch of perfection.

I am that pitch
I am that perfection.

Papa's a civilian again, mother is coiled in a corset,
Dispenses perfection with:

Castor oil
Tapestry
Tablecloths (white)
Rectal thermometers
Czerny and prunes
Sonatinas of Hummel
The white meat of chicken
The white meat of fish
The maids and the lost silver.

Lord, I am good for nothing, shall never know want.

Blinded, I burn, am led not into temptation.

The home is the centre of power.
                              There I reign
Childless. Three daughters, all whores, all —

Should be devoured by the fires of Gehenna
Should be dissolved in the womb that bore them
Should wander the wastelands forever.

Instead, they dance.

Whole towns condemn me. Flames from the roofs
Form my father's fiery image. He waves, laughs,

Cools his head among stars, leaves me shorn,
Without sons, unsanctified, biting on

Bread of affliction. Naked, I burn,
Orphaned again in a war.

The world is a different oyster:
Mine.

His defection will not be forgotten.

Blessed be He whose law speaks of the three different
          characters of children whom
we are to instruct on this occasion:

What says the wicked one?

'What do you all mean by this?'
This thou shalt ask not, and thou hast transgressed, using
          you and excluding thyself.

Thou shalt not exclude thyself from:

The collective body of the family
The collective body of the race
The collective body of the nation

Therefore repeat after me:

'This is done because of what the Eternal did
For me when I came forth from Egypt.'

The wicked wants always the last word (for all the good
It does): 'Had I been there, I would still not be worth

My redemption.' Nothing more may be eaten, a beating
     will
Take place in the laundry. Naked.

'Honour thy father and thy mother'

What says the wise one?

'The testimonies, statutes, the judgments delivered by
     God
I accept.'

Nonetheless, though thou are wise,
After the paschal offering there shall be no dessert.

'Honour thy father and thy mother'

What says the simple one?

Asks merely: 'What is this?'
Is told: 'With might of hand

Did our God bring us forth out of Egypt
From the mansion of bondage.'

Any more questions? Ask away and be damned.

'Honour thy father and thy mother'

FAY ZWICKY

Yisborach, v'yistabach, v'yispoar, v'yisroman, v'yisnaseh,
v'yishaddor, v'yisalleh, v'yishallol, sh'meh d'kudsho,
b'rich hu

Praise death who is our God
Live for death who is our God
Die for death who is our God
Blessed be your failure which is our God

Oseh sholom bim'romov, hu yaaseh sholom, olenu
v'al kol yisroel, v'imru O

_____

And he who was never born and has not the capacity to
inquire shall say:

There is a time to speak
and a time to be silent
There is a time to forgive
and a time in which to be
Forgiven.
After forgiveness,

Silence.

RANDOLPH STOW

b. 1935

Before Eden

I, Lucifer, informed with fire,
rebellious son whom only darkness loves,
grew tired of heaven. The everlasting choir
rehearsals and the conscientious doves,
the sighing streams, the flowers, the fields, the trees
—it was too much. For months, yes, or a year
perhaps, but not forever. Things like these
make good vacations, but a dull career.

Moloch and Belial, Beelzebub and I,
insurgent and forever hateful crew,
discussed the matter and rebelled. The sky
took fire from seraph-wings; all heaven through
blest conscripts (not a cherub was exempt)
rose to chastise. This done, He read His ban;
and in His fierce and beautiful contempt,
that we might know ourselves, created Man.

GARRY GEDDES

b. 1940

Word

I became flesh, I swam,
impatient, in placental
waters. Rubber gloves
guided my lethal skull
into the breach, launched
me into thinner seas.
A quart of good champagne
splashed down my side,
a tiny motor propelled
me forward.

Ship after ship went
down, the screams
of men meant nothing.
I sang in the air, my song
shattered a child's thought.
They planted me in fields,
under bridges, no one
collected the pieces.
They dropped me on cities,
the charred flesh stuck
in my throat.

They updated me, made me
streamlined and beautiful.
I grew vain. My lust could
not be glutted. I turned on them.
They spoke of God, of honour.
I wiped my mouth
on my sleeve.

ALAN ALEXANDER

b. 1941

Bruno

'It is unity that doth enchant me.'
— Giordano The Nolan

Dogs bark in February, in the Square
Of Flowers it is icy cold, the ice
Settles on the people like a promise.
Of ectasy, pickpocket and beggar
Mingle, working the fringes of the crowd
Like practised brothers, scrofulous and shrewd.

'Some say he hath recanted. Can it be?
Named his errors? God's death on it, I am
Frozen for his courtesy. He did seem
Ambitious as any lover. — They say
His notions pour forth unashamed, my lord;
He is to burn. His judges have accord.'

Tactless, insane in social relations,
Passed on by Europe's princes with a gift,
Giordano the Ginger-Bearded, left
With his own starred enchantment, rises, shuns
The clerics of St. John inside his cell,
Thinking of Love, the object of his will.

And so from the Nona Tower, the prisoner
Nude, fastened to a stake, appears; and those
Whose skullcaps crown the pallor of the rose,
Moving with solemn tread and chanted prayer.
'Let the wretch roast. — A pox on heresy; —
Expel the Devil. — Leave your errancy.'

ALAN ALEXANDER

Supreme morning of the spirit, amor
Dei intellectualis; the man
Dreams of infinite worlds, deathless matter
Lost in unfolding form, sun beyond sun:
Seeing, within the whiteness of the fire,
The singing phoenix of his one desire.

DEREK MAHON

b. 1941

Matthew V, 29-30

Lord, mine eye offended
So I plucked it out.
Imagine my chagrin

When the offence continued.
So I plucked out
The other, but

The offence continued.
In the dark now, and
Working by touch, I shaved

My head. The offence continued.
Removed an ear,
Another, dispatched the nose,

The offence continued.
Imagine my chagrin.
Next, in long strips, the skin —

Razored the tongue, the toes,
The personal nitty-gritty.
The offence continued.

But now, the thing
Finding its own momentum,
The more so since

The offence continued,
I entered upon
A prolonged course

Of lobotomy and vivisection.
Reducing the self
To a rubble of organs,

A wreckage of bones
In ᵗhe midst of which, somewhere,
The offence continued.

Quicklime, then, for the
Calcium, paraquat
For the unregenerate offal,

A spreading of topsoil,
A ploughing of this
And a sowing of it with barley.

Paraffin for the records
Of birth, flu
And abortive scholarship.

For the whimsical postcards,
The cheques
Dancing like hail,

The surviving copies
Of poems published
And unpublished. A scalpel

For the casual turns
Of phrase engraved
On the minds of others.

A chemical spray
For the stray
Thoughts hanging in the air,

For the people
who breathed them in.
Sadly, therefore, deletion

Of the many people
From their desks, beds,
Breakfasts, buses.

Tandems and catamarans.
Deletion of their
Machinery and architecture,

All evidence whatever
Of civility and reflection
Of laughter and tears.

Destruction of all things on which
That reflection fed,
Of vegetable and bird,

Erosion of all rocks
From the holiest mountain
To the least stone,

Evaporation of all seas,
The extinction of heavenly bodies —
Until, at last, offence

Was not to be found
In that silence without bound.
Only then was I fit for human society.

ANTONIO CISNEROS

b. 1942

On the Death of the Bishop
Who Was Truly of Your Ilk

Lord, your accomplice
the bishop is dead.
Some old women
are weeping
among muted bells
& his debtors
observe joyful
mourning.
Lord, he was truly
your friend,
& at the business table
you worried
about his deals.
In the old days
you stuffed your chests
with Abel's things.
I also suspect
you knowingly
sent Jesus
to the slaughter-house.

(trans. Maureen Ahern and David Tipton)

PAUL MURRAY

b. 1947

Introit

This morning,
on entering the cold chapel,

       I looked first
to the sun, as the pagan does;
not by strict custom
nor by restraint,

       I too, as creature,
sense man's primitive emotion:
his need to praise.
And so, like priest or pagan,

       according
as the sun moves, I perform
this ancient ritual.
And though not always able

       to approach,
often, effaced in light, I stand
before this
chalice of the morning,

       I break this
ordinary bread as something holy.

PAUL MURRAY

Lauds

All things the Lord has made, O bless the Lord,
Give glory and eternal praise to Him . . .

Together with our morning papers' dead:
unsmiling heroes, war-jaded, no longer game, the old,
the maimed, you also, your stoic gaiety
now needed more than ritual,

        O bless the Lord.

And you, and you also,
crazed victims of unnatural love, chained to
the masks of vampire or sacrificial dove,
the tortured and the torturer,

        O bless the Lord.

And you, who have no fear
of those who crush the bone, your innocence inviolable;
stone angel, prostrate in your mother's womb,
unwanted three-months' miracle,

        O bless the Lord.

And buried behind charitable walls,
the unseen, unmourned for, you, your voices ever singing
in the darkness, cherubim of dwarf and mongol, bright
galaxy of souls of Limbo,

        O bless the Lord.

And you, the hideously mourned, lips
parted, rouge, smiling under expensive oils, O Dives,
when through the painted mask
your lips are burned,

        O bless the Lord.

And you, when on your brow there glows
the desolate mark of Cain, when in your eyes, in the
  temple
of your heart, only the towering and dead
effigies of God remain.

        O bless the Lord.

PAUL MURRAY

And you, whose memory revives
after the serpent sting: eyes closed, imagining your soul
redeemed, re-entering the lost kingdom. Exile,
when Death shall prove your dream,

O bless the Lord.
And you, those dying under ritual of torture
or no ritual: the suicides, the uncremated spirits in the
    fires
of Purgatory and Buchenwald, — O quiet, innumerable
souls facing unquiet doom,

now, out of the burning fiery furnace,
out of the heart of the flame,

give glory and eternal praise to Him.

ANDREW LANSDOWN

b. 1954

The Woman Who Found the Well (John 4)

Why, it was as if He lowered
a pail into the well of my soul
and brought it back brimming with secrets.
All the time
My waters rose to Him
And I told Him things He already knew
because He first asked
of me a drink — I a Samaritan
and He a Jew.

And *He* offered *me* a Drink,
said I should thirst
no more.
I said, You have nothing to draw
with; and the well is deep.
This caused Him to repeat
His mystery:
A well of living water within you,
springing up.

For a moment I mistook His meaning —
thought I'd not have to come
to the well again
in the dust and heat
after the other women had come and gone.

ACKNOWLEDGEMENTS

For permission to reprint the poems in this anthology, acknowledgement is made to the following:

A. D. Peters & Co. Ltd for Frank O'Connor's 'The Priest Rediscovers His Psalm Book', 'The Sweetness of Nature' and 'Ireland v Rome' and for Anne Sexton's 'For God While Sleeping'.

Alfred A. Knopf, Inc., for Langston Hughes's 'Madam and the Minister' from his *Selected Poems*.

Andre Deutsch and Rapp & Whiting for John Haines's 'The Wreck' from *The Stone Harp* and for Geoffrey Hill's 'Lachrimae Verae' and 'Lachrimae Amantis' from *Tenebrae.*

Angus & Robertson for Gwen Harwood's 'Triste, Triste' from her *Selected Poems;* for James McAuley's 'Late Sunday Afternoon' and 'Jesus' from his *Collected Poems;* for Francis Webb's 'Five Days Old' from his *Collected Poems;* for Randolph Stow's 'Before Eden' from his *A Counterfeit Silence;* for Judith Wright's 'Eli, Eli' from her *Collected Poems 1942-1970.*

A. P. Watt Ltd, Macmillan Co. of London & Basingstoke and M. B. Yeats for W. B. Yeats's 'An Irish Airman Forsees his Death', 'The Mother of God' and 'The Second Coming' from his *Collected Poems.*

Behrman House, New York, for A. M. Klein's 'The Still Small Voice' from *Hath Not a Jew* .

Charles Scribner's Sons, New York, for 'Fancy' from *Words* by Robert Creeley. Copyright © 1967 Robert Creeley.

Chatto & Windus Ltd and the author for Richard Eberhart's 'If I could only live at the pitch that is near madness'; and Chatto & Windus and The Owen Estate for poems by Wilfred Owen.

Faber & Faber Ltd for John Berryman's No. 153 and No. 156 from 'The Dream Songs' in *His Toy, His Dream,*

ACKNOWLEDGEMENTS

His Rest; for T. S. Eliot's 'Journey of the Magi', 'The Cultivation of Christmas Trees' from *Collected Poems 1909 — 1962;* for Ted Hughes' 'Crow's Theology', 'Crow Blacker than ever' from *Crow;* for W. H. Auden's 'We demand a Miracle' from 'For the Time Being' in his *Collected Poems;*
Thom Gunn's 'Jesus and His Mother' from *The Sense of Movement;* for 'A Short Prayer to Mary', 'Jesus, my Sweet Lover' and 'Pleasure it is' from *Medieval English Lyrics* edited by R. T. Davies; for Randall Jarrell's 'The Orient Express' from his *Complete Poems;* for Edwin Muir's 'The Killing' and 'In Love for Long' from *The Collected Poems of Edwin Muir;* for Philip Larkin's 'Days' and 'Arundel Tomb' from his *The Whitsun Weddings;* for David Jones's 'A,a,a, Domine Deus' from *The Sleeping Lord;* for Anne Ridler's 'Christmas and Common Birth' from *The Nine Bright Shiners;* for Robert Lowell's 'Our Lady of Walsingham' from *Poems 1938-1949;* for Marianne Moore's 'What Are Years?', from *The Complete Poems of Marianne Moore;* for Theodore Roethke's 'What Can I Tell My Bones?'
Fremantle Arts Centre Press, Western Australia, for Alan Alexander's 'Bruno' from *In the Sun's Eye.*
Gary Geddes of Concordia University, Montreal, for his poem 'Word'.
Geoffrey Chapman, a division of Cassell Ltd, for E. Colledge's translation of 'The Dream of the Rood' and for Jerome Kiely's 'For a Young Cistercian Monk' from *The Griffon Sings.*
Granada Publishing Ltd and MacGibbon & Kee Ltd for poems by E. E. Cummings; and Granada Publishing Ltd and Rupert Hart-Davis for R. S. Thomas' 'In a Country Church' and 'Kneeling'.
William Hart-Smith for his poem 'Eathelswith' which first appeared in Quadrant Magazine, Sydney, Australia.
Harvard University Press for Emily Dickinson's poems 1791, 1732 and 501 from *The Poems of Emily Dickinson.*

191

ACKNOWLEDGEMENTS

Harvill Press Ltd for Roy Campbell's translation of 'Concerning the Divine Word' and 'Upon a Gloomy Night'.

J. M. Dent & Sons Ltd and the Trustees for the Copyrights of the late Dylan Thomas for Dylan Thomas's 'And Death Shall Have No Dominion' from his *Collected Poems*.

Johns Hopkins University Press for Sidney Lanier's 'A Ballad of Trees and the Master' from *Centennial Edition of Works of Sidney Lanier,* Charles R. Andersen ed. © 1945 The Johns Hopkins Press; for Henry David Thoreau's 'Light winged smoke, Icarian Bird' and 'Great God I ask thee no meaner pelf' from Carl Bode, *The Collected Poems of Henry Thoreau* © 1970 by Carl Bode.

The widow of Patrick Kavanagh for 'Pegasus' and 'To be Dead'.

Andrew Lansdown of Western Australia for his poem 'The Woman Who Found the Well'.

Laurence Polliger Ltd and the Estate of the late Mrs Frieda Lawrence Ravagli for D. H. Lawrence's 'Phoenix' and 'Pax' from *The Complete Poems of D. H. Lawrence* published by William Heinemann Ltd.

Longman Cheshire Pty Ltd for Bruce Dawe's 'And a Good Friday Was Had by All' from *A Need of Similar Name*.

Mr James McGibbon, as executor and Allen Lane, for Stevie Smith's 'The Weak Monk' and 'The Heavenly City'.

Macmillan and David Higham Associates Ltd for Dame Edith Sitwell's 'Still Falls the Rain' from her *Collected Poems*.

Macmillan, London and Basingstoke, and the Trustees of the Tagore Estate for Rabindranath Tagore's 'Leave this chanting and singing and telling of beads!' from *Gitanjali*.

Martin Secker & Warburg Ltd., for Gunter Grass's 'Hymn' from *In the Egg and Other Poems.*
Melbourne University Press for Vincent Buckley's 'Places' from *Arcady and Other Places.*
Methuen & Co. Ltd for Brian Higgins's 'Genesis' from *The Northern Fiddler.*

Liam Miller at the Dolmen Press, Dublin, for James Carney's translation 'The Questions of Ethne Alba.'
Paul Murray, O.P., of Dublin and the New Writer's Press for 'Introit', and the poet for 'Lauds'.
New Directions Publishing Corporation, New York, for Robert Duncan's 'The Ballad of Mrs Noah' from *The Opening of the Field,* copyright © by Robert Duncan; for Hilda Doolittle's 'The Mysteries Remain' from her *Selected Poems,* copyright © 1957 by Norman Holmes Pearson; for Rainer Maria Rilke's 'You, neighbour God, if sometimes in the night' from *Poems From the Book of Hours,* translated by Babette Deutsch, copyright © 1941 by New Directions Publishing Corporation.
Oxford University Press for Derek Mahon's 'Matthew V, 29-30 from *The Snow Party,* 1975; for John Ormond's 'To a Nun' from *Definition of a Waterfall,* 1973; for Peter Porter's 'At Whitechurch Canonicorum' from *The Last of England* 1970.
Price Milburn for James Baxter's 'From Autumn Testament'.
F. T. Prince for his poem 'The Question', and to Anvil Press, the Menard Press and the Sheep Meadow Press (New York).
G. T. Sassoon for Siegfried Sassoon's 'Stand to: Good Friday Morning'.
F. R. Scott for his poem 'Bonne Entente' and for his father F. G. Scott's poem, 'The Sting of Death'.
S.C.M., London, for lines beginning 'Once in a saintly passion' from T. E. Jessop's *Law and Love,* SCM Press 1940.

ACKNOWLEDGEMENTS

The Society of Authors as the literary representatives of the Estate of John Masefield for an extract from 'The Everlasting Mercy'; The Society of Authors as the literary representative of the Estate of A. E. Housman, and Jonathan Cape Ltd, publishers of A. E. Housman's *Collected Poems* for 'Oh Who is that Young Sinner'. David Tipton and Maureen Ahern for 'On the death of the bishop who was truly of your ilk' by Antonio Cisneros.

Gwen Watkins for Vernon Watkins's 'The Healing of the Leper'.

Fay Zwicky, Western Australia, for her poem 'Kaddish'.

ACKNOWLEDGEMENTS

INDEX OF FIRST LINES

HAROLD BRIDGES LIBRARY
S. MARTIN'S COLLEGE
LANCASTER